American Book Company

Meeting Standards,
Exceeding Expectations

MW00718159

Dear Educator,

Thank you for your interest in American Book Company's state-specific test preparation resources. We commend you for your interest in pursuing your students' success. Feel free to contact us with any questions about our books, software, or the ordering process.

Our Products Feature	Your Students Will Improve
Multiple-choice and open-ended diagnostic tests	Confidence and mastery of subjects
Step-by-step instruction	Concept development
Frequent practice exercises	Critical thinking
Chapter reviews	Test-taking skills
Multiple-choice practice tests	Problem-solving skills

American Book Company's writers and curriculum specialists have over 100 years of combined teaching experience, working with students from kindergarten through middle, high school, and adult education.

Our company specializes in effective test preparation books and software for high stakes graduation and grade promotion exams across the country.

How to Use This Book

Each book:

*contains a chart of standards which correlates all test questions and chapters to the state exam's standards and benchmarks as published by the state department of education. This chart is found in the front of all preview copies and in the front of all answer keys.

*begins with a full-length pretest (diagnostic test). This test not only adheres to your specific state standards, but also mirrors your state exam in weights and measures to help you assess each individual student's strengths and weaknesses.

*offers an evaluation chart. Depending on which questions the students miss, this chart points to which chapters individual students or the entire class need to review to be prepared for the exam.

*provides comprehensive review of all tested standards within the chapters. Each chapter includes engaging instruction, practice exercises, and chapter reviews to assess students' progress.

*finishes with two full-length practice tests for students to get comfortable with the exam and to assess their progress and mastery of the tested standards and benchmarks.

While we cannot guarantee success, our products are designed to provide students with the concept and skill development they need for the graduation test or grade promotion exam in their own state. We look forward to hearing from you soon.

Sincerely,

The American Book Company Team

PO Box 2638 ★ Woodstock, GA 30188-1383 ★ Phone: 1-888-264-5877 ★ Fax: 1-866-827-3240

Georgia 4 CRCT Social Studies Standards Chart

Georgia 4 CRCT Social Studies

Chart of Standards

The following chart correlates each question on the Diagnostic Test, Practice Test 1, and Practice Test 2 to the Georgia 4 CRCT competency goals *standards and benchmarks published by the Georgia Department of Education*. These test questions are also correlated with chapters in *Georgia 4 CRCT Social Studies*.

Chapter Number	Diagnostic Test Questions	Practice Test 1 Questions	Practice Test 2 Questions
Historical Understandings			
SS4H1 The student will describe how early Native American cultures developed in North America. a. Locate where the American Indians settled with emphasis on Arctic (Inuit), Northwest (Kwakiutl), plateu (Nez Perce), Southwest (Hopi), Plains (Pawnee), and Southeastern (Seminole). b. Describe how the American Indians used their environment to obtain food, clothing, and shelter..			
1	1, 2, 3, 19, 27, 48, 58, 66	10, 14, 23, 26, 36, 46, 58	11, 26, 34, 39
SS4H2 The student will describe European exploration in North America. a. Describe the reasons for, obstacles to, and accomplishments of the Spanish, French, and English explorations of John Cabot, Vasco Nunez Balboa, Juan Ponce de Leon, Christopher Columbus, Henry Hudson, and Jacquez Cartier. b. Describe examples of cooperation and conflict between Europeans and Nastive Americans.			
1	15, 30, 49, 62, 70	1, 2, 3, 24, 52, 63	16, 22, 45, 56, 63
SS4H3 The student will explain the factors that shaped British colonial America. a. Compare and contrast life in the New England, Mid-Atlantic, and Southern colonies. b. Describe colonial life in America as experienced by various people, including large landowners, farmers, artisans, women, indentured servants, slaves, and Native Americans.			
1	14, 34, 41, 44, 53, 67	9, 32, 49	1, 2, 3, 29, 42, 64

Standards Chart

Chapter Number	Diagnostic Test Questions	Practice Test 1 Questions	Practice Test 2 Questions
SS4H4 The student will explain the causes, events, and results of the American Revolution.			
a. Trace the events that shaped the revolutionary movement in America, including the French and Indian War, British Imperial policy that led to the 1765 Stamp Ace, the slogan "no taxation without representation," the activities of the Sons of Liberty, and the Boston Tea Party			
b. Explain the writing of the Declaration of Independence; include who wrote it, how it was written, why it was necessary, and how it was a response to tyranny and the abuse of power.			
c. Describe the major events of the Revolution and xplain the factors leading to American victory and British defeat; include the Battles of Lexington and Concord and Yorktown..			
d. Describe key individuals in the American Revolution with the emphasis on King George III, George Washington, Benjamin Franklin, Thomas Jefferson, Benedict Arnold, Patrick Henry, and John Adams .			
2	23, 39, 60, 68	12, 34, 53, 67	9, 17, 32, 46, 67, 69
SS4H5 The student will analyze the challenges faced by the new nation.			
a. Identify the weaknesses of the government established by the Articles of Confederation.			
b. Identify the major leaders of the Constitutional Convention (James Madison and Benjamin Franklin) and describe the major issues they debated, including the rights of states, the Great Compromise, and slavery.			
c. Identify the three branches of the US government as outlined by the Constitution, describe what they do, how they relate to each other (checks and balances and separation of power), and how they relate to the states.			
d. Identify and explain the rights in the Bill off Rights, describe how the Bill of Rights places limits on the power of government, and explain the reasons for its inclusion in the Constitution in 1791.			
e. Describe the causes of the War of 1812; include burning of the Capitol and the White House.			
3	9, 24, 40, 69	15, 30, 37, 42, 54, 65, 68	14, 20, 35, 47, 54, 57, 61, 62, 68
SS4H6 The student will explain westward expansion of America between 1801 and 1861.			
a. Describe territorial expansion with emphasis on the Louisiana Purchase, the Lewis and Clark expedition, and the Acquisitions of Texas (the Alamo and independence), Oregon (Oregon Trail), and California (Gold Rush and the development of mining towns).			
b. Describe the impact of the steamboat, the steam locomotive, and the telegraph on life in America.			
4	8, 25, 42, 54	18, 21, 50, 61	8, 41, 43, 51
SS4H7 The student will examine the main ideas of the abolitionist and suffrage movements.			
a. Discuss biographies of Harriet Tubman and Elizabeth Cady Stanton.			
b. Explain the significance of Sojourner Truth's address ("Ain't I a Woman?" 1851) to the Ohio Women's Rights Convention.			
4	11, 32, 55	5, 39, 47, 57	4, 27

Georgia 4 CRCT Social Studies

Chapter Number	Diagnostic Test Questions	Practice Test 1 Questions	Practice Test 2 Questions
Geographic Understandings			
SS4G1 The student will be able to locate important physical and man-made features in the United States.			
a. Locate major physical features of the United States; include the Atlantic Coastal Plain, Great Plains, Continental Divide, the Great Basin, Death Valley, Gulf of Mexico, St. Lawrence River, and the Great Lakes.			
b. Locate major man-made features; include New York City, NY; Boston, MA; Philadelphia, PA; and the Erie Canal.			
5	10, 26, 33, 45, 65	4, 20, 40, 55, 56, 64	13, 28, 40, 48, 58
SS4G2 The student will describe how physical systems affect human systems.			
a. Explain why each of the native American groups (SS4H1a) occupied the areas they did, with emphasis on why some developed permanent villages and others did not.			
b. Describe how the early explorers (SS4H2a) adapted, or failed to adapt, to the various physical environments in which they traveled.			
c. Explain how the physical geography of each colony helped determine economic activities practiced therin.			
d. Explain how each force (American and British) attempted to use the physical geography of each battle site to its benefit (SS4H4c).			
e. Describe physical barriers that hindered and physical gateways that benefited territorial expansion from 1801 to 1861 (SS4H6a).			
5	4, 20, 38, 52, 56, 61	6, 25, 27, 45	5, 23, 25, 38
Government/Civic Understandings			
SS4CG1 The student will describe the meaning of			
a. Natural rights as found in the Declaration of Independence (the right to life, liberty and the pursuit of happiness).			
b. "We the people" from the Preamble to the US Constitution as a reflection of consent of the governed or popular sovereignty.			
c. The federal system of government in the US.			
6	12, 28, 47, 63	7, 19, 28, 38, 48, 59, 69	6, 21, 36, 49, 59
SS4CG2 The student will explain the importance of freedom of expression as written in the First Amendment to the US Constitution.			
6	17, 35	13, 66	10, 59, 70

Standards Chart

Chapter Number	Diagnostic Test Questions	Practice Test 1 Questions	Practice Test 2 Questions
SS4CG3 The student will describe the functions of government.			
a. Explain the process for making and enforcing laws.			
b. Explain managing conflicts and protecting rights.			
c. Describe providing for the defense of the nation.			
d. Explain limiting the power of people in authority.			
e. Explain the fiscal responsibility of government.			
6	7, 22, 31, 46, 57	16, 22, 31, 43, 60	15, 18, 31, 50, 65
SS4CG4 The student will explain the importance of Americans sharing certain central democratic beliefs and principles, both personal and civic.			
a. Explain the necessity of respecting the rights of others and promoting the common good.			
b. Explain the necessity of obeying reasonable laws/rules voluntarily, and explain why it is important for citizens in a democratic society to participate in public officials).			
c. Describe providing for the defense of the nation.			
d. Explain limiting the power of people in authority.			
e. Explain the fiscal responsibility of government.			
6	16, 36, 51	11, 41, 51	19, 44
SS4CG5 The student will name positive character traits of key historic figures and government leaders (honesty, patriotism, courage, trustworthiness).			
6	18	33	30
Economic Understandings			
SS4E1 The student will use the basic economic concepts of trade, opportunity cost, specialization, voluntary exchange, productivity, and price incentives to illustrate historical events.			
a. Describe opportunity costs and their relationship to decision-making across time (such as decisions to send expeditions to the New World).			
b. Explain how price incentives affect people's behavior and choices (such as colonial decisions about what crops to grow and products to produce.			
c. Describe how specialization improves standards of living (such as how specific economies in the three colonial regions developed).			
d. Explain how voluntary exchange helps both buyers and sellers (such as prehistoric and colonial trade in North America).			
e. Describe how trade promotes economic activity (such as how trade activities in the early nation were managed differently under the Articles of Confederation and the Constitution).			
f. Give examples of technological advancements and their impact on business productivity during the development of the United States.			
7	13, 29, 37, 50, 64	8, 29, 44, 62, 70	7, 24, 37, 52, 60, 66
SS4E2 The student will identify the elements of a personal budget and explain why personal spending and saving decisions are important.			
7	6, 21, 43, 59	17, 35	12, 33, 53

American Book Company's

MASTERING THE GEORGIA

4TH GRADE

CRCT

IN

SOCIAL STUDIES

Developed to the Georgia Performance Standards

Kindred Howard
Katie Herman
Amy Fletcher
Cindy L. Rex
Elaine E. Schneider

American Book Company
PO Box 2638
Woodstock, GA 30188-1383
Toll Free: 1 (888) 264-5877   Phone: (770) 928-2834
Fax: (770) 928-7483   Toll Free Fax: 1 (866) 827-3240
www.americanbookcompany.com

ACKNOWLEDGEMENTS

The authors would like to gratefully acknowledge the formatting and technical contributions of Marsha Torrens and Yvonne Benson.

We also want to thank Charisse Johnson and Eric Field for developing the graphics for this book.

This product/publication includes images from CorelDRAW 9 and 11 which are protected by the copyright laws of the United States, Canada, and elsewhere. Used under license.

Chapter2 The American Revolution   **39**

Chapter 3 The New Nation   **51**

PREFACE

Georgia 4th Grade CRCT in Social Studies will help students who are learning or reviewing material for the CRCT. The materials in this book are based on the testing standards as published by the Georgia Department of Education.

This book contains several sections. These sections are as follows: 1) general information about the book; 2) a diagnostic test; 3) an evaluation chart; 4) chapters that teach the concepts and skills that improve graduation readiness; 5) two practice tests. Answers to the tests and exercises are in a separate manual. The answer manual also contains a Chart of Standards for teachers to make a more precise diagnosis of student needs and assignments.

We welcome comments and suggestions about the book. Please contact the author at

American Book Company
PO Box 2638
Woodstock, GA 30188-1383

Toll Free: 1 (888) 264-5877
Phone: (770) 928-2834
Fax: (770) 928-7483
Web site: www.americanbookcompany.com

ABOUT THE AUTHORS

Lead Author:

Kindred Howard is a 1991 alumnus of the University of North Carolina at Chapel Hill, where he graduated with a B.S. in Criminal Justice and national honors in Political Science. In addition to two years as a probation & parole officer in North Carolina, he has served for over twelve years as a teacher and writer in the fields of religion and social studies. His experience includes teaching students at both the college and high school level, as well as speaking at numerous seminars. He is the author of several books on US history, American government, and economics. His books are currently used by public schools in Georgia, the Carolinas, Louisiana, and Maryland. In 2005, Mr. Howard received a national recognition of excellence for scoring in the top fifteen percent, all time, on the national Praxis II exam for social studies. He currently serves as the social studies coordinator for American Book Company and is completing a M.A. in history at Georgia State University. Mr. Howard lives in Kennesaw, Georgia, with his wife and three children.

Katie Herman is a graduate of Kennesaw State University, where she received a B.A. in English. She is the co-author of several books on history and social studies, which are currently being used by public schools in Georgia and Louisiana. Ms. Herman currently works as a researcher and writer for American Book Company and plans to pursue a M.A. in professional writing. She lives in Woodstock, Georgia.

Amy Fletcher is a 2001 graduate of Brewton-Parker College in Mt. Vernon, Georgia, where she graduated with a B.S. in Early Childhood Education. She spent three years teaching elementary school before becoming an educational writer and stay-at-home mom. Her experience also includes directing and speaking at leadership conferences. She has authored children's fiction for magazine publication, and works with educational materials for grades K-8. Mrs. Fletcher lives in West Green, Georgia, with her husband and three children.

Cindy L. Rex is a 1984 alumnus of the University of Michigan-Flint. She graduated with a B.S. in Social Studies and Education and is a member of the education honor society, Kappa Delta Pi. In addition to a M.A. from Marygrove College, Detroit, she has 30 graduate credits from Eastern Michigan University in English. Her experience includes 24 years as a teacher and six years as a volleyball coach at LakeVille Middle School in Otisville, MI. She is also Head Teacher of the middle school building and the grade level Lead Teacher. She has been a constituent of the Michigan Educational Assessment Program as a team review member and the Item Writing Team (IWT), and was awarded a Fulbright Teacher Exchange for the 2008-2009 school year. Cindy lives in Birch Run, MI.

Elaine E. Schneider is a teacher and published author of several articles. As a freelance curriculum writer she has worked with several major educational companies and is the managing editor of Lesson Tutor, an educational website.

Georgia 4 Social Studies Diagnostic Test

The purpose of this diagnostic test is to measure your knowledge in social studies. This test is based on the GPS-based Georgia CRCT in Social Studies and adheres to the sample question format provided by the Georgia Department of Education.

General Directions:

1. Read all directions carefully.

2. Read each question or sample. Then choose the best answer.

3. Choose only one answer for each question. If you change an answer, be sure to erase your original answer completely.

4. After taking the test, you or your instructor should score it using the evaluation chart following the test. Circle any questions you did not get correct and review those chapters.

Use the map below to answer questions 1 to 3.

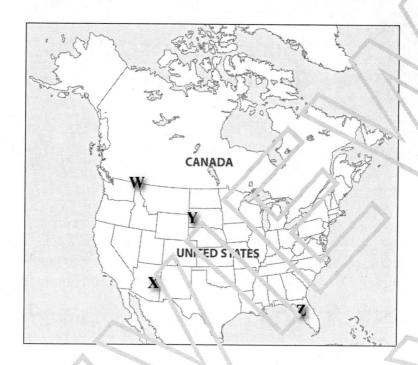

1. Which area shown on the map was home to the Pawnee? SS4H1
   A. W   B. X   C. Y   D. Z

2. Which area on the map represents where the Seminoles lived? SS4H1
   A. W   B. X   C. Y   D. Z

3. Which area on the map was home to the Hopi? SS4H1
   A. W   B. X   C. Y   D. Z

4. The United States' first president was SS4H4
   A. Thomas Jefferson
   B. Abraham Lincoln
   C. George Washington
   D. John Adams

5. Which of the following made early westward expansion harder? SS4G2
   A. Cumberland Gap
   B. Missouri River
   C. Rocky Mountains
   D. Louisiana Purchase

6. What is the **best** heading for the list below? SS4E2
   - Education
   - People could lose their job.
   - Being ready for financial challenges.

   A. Reasons to Save Money

   B. Reasons People go Into Debt

   C. Causes for Increased Income

   D. Reasons to Spend Money

7. The US Congress is divided into two houses. Which house consists of two representatives from each state, no matter what the population of the state? SS4CG3

   A. the House of Representatives

   B. the Senate

   C. the president's Cabinet

   D. judicial branch

8. In 1849, large numbers of people rushed to California because SS4H6

   A. they were looking for oil.

   B. they were hiding from violent Native Americans.

   C. they wanted to get rich from gold.

   D. they were forced to leave the South because of a drought.

9. The legislative branch of government is responsible for SS4H5

   A. making laws.

   B. enforcing laws.

   C. making sure laws follow the Constitution.

   D. organizing trials.

10. Features built by humans are called SS4G1

    A. physical features.

    B. geographical features.

    C. man-made features.

    D. natural features.

11. Who is **most** associated with the Underground Railroad? SS4H

    A. Elizabeth Cady Stanton

    B. William Clark

    C. Harriet Tubman

    D. Sojourner Truth

12. The federal government is responsible for SS4CG1

    A. public education.

    B. carrying on foreign trade.

    C. regulating licenses.

    D. overseeing elections.

13. When producers freely choose to sell and consumers freely choose to buy, it is called SS4E1

    A. competition.

    B. a closed market.

    C. voluntary exchange.

    D. specialization.

14. What is the list below describing? SS4H3

    - worked for landowners for up to seven years

    - eventually gained their freedom and owned land

    - often treated cruelly by their masters

    A. slavery

    B. indentured servants

    C. Puritan life

    D. Quakers

15. Settlements established by a country in a foreign land are called SS4H2

    A. outposts.

    B. colonies.

    C. journies.

    D. missions.

16. Kelly wants Barack Obama to be president. On Election Day, she will choose him in favor of John McCain. Kelly plans to participate in her government by SS4CG4

    A. volunteering.

    B. exercising her freedom to assemble

    C. obeying her fiscal responsibility

    D. voting.

17. Citizens and news agencies may print what they want as long as they don't violate someone else's rights. This is called SS4CG2

    A. freedom of the press.

    B. freedom to assemble.

    C. limited government.

    D. concurrent powers.

18. Good leaders should care more about their country than they do about themselves. This is called SS4CG5

    A. honesty.

    B. communication.

    C. patriotism.

    D. courage.

19. Where did the Seminoles live?   SS4H1

    A. southeastern United States

    B. Oregon and Washington

    C. Midwest Plains

    D. arctic regions

20. In the early 1700s, the Appalachian Mountains, the Mississippi River, and the Rocky Mountains were   SS4G2

    A. home to many colonial settlements.

    B. obstacles to expansion.

    C. easy to navigate and cross.

    D. owned by the United States.

21. If Jack wants to be sure that he spends less money than he makes, then he should   SS4E2

    A. borrow money.

    B. trade goods.

    C. make a budget.

    D. go into debt.

22. An example of a military force that helps protect the US is   SS4CG3

    A. the Supreme Court.

    B. the Marine Corps.

    C. the president.

    D. Congress.

23. The last major battle of the American Revolution was   SS4H4

    A. Saratoga.

    B. Yorktown.

    C. Trenton.

    D. Princeton.

24. The US Bill of Rights   SS4H_

    A. was the first part of the US Constitution written.

    B. is made up of ten amendments to the Constitution that protect citizens' rights.

    C. upset people who believed in personal freedoms.

    D. includes the Twelfth through the Nineteenth Amendments.

Read the passage below and answer the following question.

> In 1836, nearly 200 Texans bravely faced 5,000 Mexican soldiers. After 13 days, General Santa Anna's soldiers stormed the little church's walls. The battle was over, and the freedom fighters all lay dead. The story would become a legend in Texas and American history.

25. What is the passage above describing?   SS4H6

   A. Lexington and Concord

   B. the Alamo

   C. the battle at Sand Creek

   D. Seneca Falls

26. Much of the Midwest is covered by a flatland prairie region called the   SS4G1

   A. Great Plains.

   B. Atlantic Coastal Plain.

   C. Great Lakes region.

   D. Continental Divide.

27. The Inuit lived in   SS4H1

   A. North Carolina.

   B. the Southwest United States.

   C. arctic regions.

   D. large cities.

28. The Declaration of Independence states that people have natural rights. Natural rights are rights that   SS4CG1

   A. guarantee happiness.

   B. come with owning property.

   C. people are born with and the government can't take away.

   D. give the government its power to rule.

29. Mary Jane wants to go shopping for new shoes. She hears about a sale at a local store and decides to go there first. What encourages her to do this?   SS4E1

   A. specialization

   B. price incentive

   C. opportunity cost

   D. name brand incentive

30. Who discovered Florida while searching for the *Fountain of Youth*?   SS4H2

   A. Vasco Nunez Balboa

   B. Henry Hudson

   C. Juan Ponce de Leon

   D. John Cabot

Use the diagram below to answer question number 31.

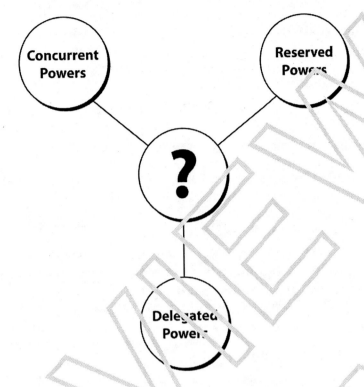

31. What does the diagram **most likely** represent?   SS4CG3

   A. vetoing a federal law

   B. the president overriding Congress

   C. making a federal law

   D. federalism

32. Which of the following   SS4H7
   demanded that women be
   allowed to vote?

   A. the suffrage movement

   B. the abolitionist movement

   C. the Sons of Liberty

   D. plantation owners

33. What city became the   SS4G1
   center of government
   during and after the American
   Revolution?

   A. Atlanta

   B. Philadelphia

   C. Boston

   D. Chicago

34. The British colonies of   SS4H3
    New York, New Jersey,
    Pennsylvania, and Delaware
    were

    A. New England Colonies.

    B. Royal Colonies.

    C. Southern Colonies.

    D. Middle Colonies.

Read the list below and answer the following question.

- Freedom of Religion
- Freedom of Speech
- Freedom of the Press
- Freedom to Assemble
- Freedom to Petition the Government

35. What is the best heading   SS4CG2
    for the list above?

    A. Rights under the Articles of Confederation

    B. Rights protected by the Twelfth Amendment

    C. Rights protected by the First Amendment

    D. Rights mentioned in the Preamble to the Constitution

36. Respecting the rights of   SS4CG4
    others and promoting the
    common good are ways that
    people

    A. participate in an election.

    B. practice positive citizenship

    C. obey laws.

    D. limit the power of leaders.

37. Early colonists who lived   SS4E1
    in the South tended to

    A. live in cities

    B. raise cash crops.

    C. own fewer slaves.

    D. belong to the Puritan church.

38. The Native Americans of   SS4G2
    the Great Plains did not
    have many natural resources, so
    they

    A. only ate fruits and vegetables.

    B. depended on others to feed them.

    C. often lived nomadic lifestyles.

    D. built permanent communities.

39. Before the Revolutionary War, colonists organized boycotts against Great Britain. What group used violence and threats to enforce these boycotts? SS4H4

    A. Sons of Liberty

    B. Massachusetts Militia

    C. Second Continental Congress

    D. Imperial Policy

40. Which of the following is a right guaranteed in the Bill of Rights? SS4H5

    A. the right to earn a minimum wage

    B. the right to carry out plots against the government

    C. the right to meet for peaceful gatherings

    D. the right to health care

41. The **main** responsibilities of colonial women were to SS4H3

    A. teach school and prepare lessons.

    B. raise children and take care of the home.

    C. serve as political leaders.

    D. run plantations and businesses.

42. How did the Louisiana Purchase contribute to western expansion? SS4H6

    A. The US owned land west of the Mississippi River.

    B. The discovery of gold in New Orleans attracted settlers.

    C. It gave the US all land east of the Mississippi River.

    D. It did not contribute to western expansion at all.

43. Rebecca makes about $2500 a month. She pays $800 a month in rent and at least $1000 a month on other things. The remaining $700 a month goes in the bank. Which of the following statements is true? SS4E2

    A. Rebecca saves over half of her income.

    B. Rebecca's expenses equal about $1800 a month.

    C. Rebecca spends more than she makes.

    D. Rebecca's expenses equal $2500 a month.

44. Juan is a Spanish   SS4H3
    explorer. In 1513, he was
    one of the first Europeans to
    reach the Pacific coast of the
    Americas. Who led his
    expedition?
    A. Christopher Columbus
    B. Samuel de Champlain
    C. Jacques Cartier
    D. Vasco Nunez Balboa

Read the list below and answer the following question.

- Largest city in the United States
- Popular arrival point for immigrants
- One of the world' major centers for business
- Located on the Atlantic coast

45. Which city is the list   SS4G1
    describing?
    A. New York
    B. Philadelphia
    C. Atlanta
    D. Detroit

46. Which branch of   SS4CG3
    government is responsi-
    ble for making sure that people
    follow the laws?
    A. legislative
    B. executive
    C. judical
    D. Congress

47. The writers of the   SS4CG1
    Constitution believed that
    the people should
    A. elect leaders to represent them.
    B. not have a voice in government.
    C. govern themselves without elected leaders
    D. be allowed to live and act however they choose.

48. If a Native American   SS4H1
    lived in southwest
    Canada, he was **most likely** a
    A. Pawnee.
    B. Kwakiutl.
    C. Seminole.
    D. Hopi.

In 1492, he sailed across the Atlantic Ocean in search of a faster way to reach Asia. On his journey, he found new land. He established Hispaniola, Spain's first permanent colony in the Americas.

49. Who of the following is the passage referring to? *SS4H2*

A. Juan Ponce de Leon

B. Christopher Columbus

C. Jacques Cartier

D. Samuel de Champlain

50. Sharon is back-to-school shopping. She wants to buy a new backpack and new notebooks. She only has enough money for one or the other. Sharon buys the notebooks. What is her opportunity cost? *SS4E1*

A. the cost of the backpack

B. the price of the notebooks

C. carrying her books in a backpack

D. the joy of having new notebooks

51. Jennifer wants to be a good citizen. She volunteers to help at a retirement home on Saturdays. This is an example of *SS4CG4*

A. obeying the law.

B. community activism.

C. staying informed.

D. freedom of speech.

52. Which of the following helped Lewis and Clark journey west? *SS4G2*

A. Missouri River

B. Rocky Mountains

C. St. Lawrence River

D. Cumberland Gap

53. In 1620, Puritans established a colony at Plymouth, Massachusetts. These settlers became known as the *SS4H3*

A. Quakers.

B. Pilgrims

C. artisans.

D. Native Americans.

Use the map below to answer question number 54.

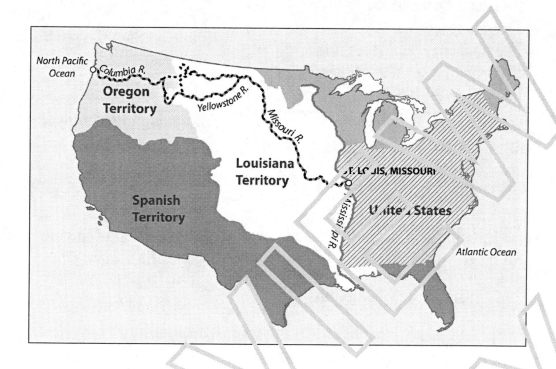

54. What does the route on the map above **most likely** show? SS4H6

A. Louisiana Purchase

B. Washington's March to Yorktown

C. the Erie Canal

D. Lewis and Clark Expedition

55. Elizabeth Cady Stanton and the Seneca Falls Conference are **most** associated with SS4H7

A. abolition.

B. western expansion.

C. women's suffrage.

D. education reform.

56. At the battle of Yorktown in 1781, what geographical feature did General George Washington use to help him win? SS4G2

A. open fields

B. the Atlantic Ocean

C. high ground

D. the Delaware River

57. Why is it important that the US have a strong national defense?   SS4CG3

    A. it is not important

    B. to provide strict punishment for US criminals

    C. to be able to defend itself

    D. so male citizens over the age of 18 can join the military

58. **All** early Native Americans **always** relied on which of the following to survive?   SS4H1

    A. their environment

    B. fishing

    C. farming

    D. nuts and berries

59. People often go into debt because they   SS4E2

    A. save all their money instead of paying bills.

    B. cannot pay back the money that they borrowed.

    C. have income that is greater than the amount they owe.

    D. stick to a budget.

60. Who does the following list describe?   SS4H4

    • Great inventor, scientist, and writer

    • helped to convince France to support America during the revolution

    A. Benjamin Franklin

    B. King George III

    C. John Adams

    D. Benedict Arnold

61. The Cumberland Gap   SS4G2

    A. made early westward expansion harder.

    B. made early westward expansion easier.

    C. did not affect westward expansion.

    D. contributed to Washington's victory at Yorktown.

62. How did Columbus treat Native Americans?   SS4H2

    A. with respect

    B. as friends

    C. He was afraid to have contact with them.

    D. He abused and enslaved them.

63. The Preamble of the US   SS4CG1
    Constitution begins with
    the words

    A. "Life, liberty, and the pursuit
       of happiness."

    B. "We the people."

    C. "Faith and credit shall be
       given to each state."

    D. "Equality of rights under the
       law shall not be denied."

64. When European nations   SS4E1
    sent explorers to the New
    World, they used money that
    could have been spent on other
    things. They decided that

    A. exploration was too risky to
       invest a lot of time or money

    B. they would only allow one
       exploration at a time.

    C. the wealth of the Americas
       made exploration worth the
       opportunity costs.

    D. the opportunity cost of giving
       up the explorations was the
       best choice.

65. The flatland area that   SS4G1
    runs along the coast of
    the Atlantic Ocean is the

    A. Great Plains.

    B. Continental Divide.

    C. Great Basin.

    D. Atlantic Coastal Plain.

66. The Columbus River Pla-   SS4H1
    teau was home to the

    A. Hopi.

    B. Pawnee.

    C. Nez Perez.

    D. Seminoles.

67. Most African Americans   SS4H3
    who lived in the British
    colonies were

    A. indentured servants.

    B. Puritans.

    C. Quakers.

    D. slaves.

68. The Declaration of   SS4H4
    Independence stated that

    A. Great Britain had ruled the
       colonies with fairness and
       equality.

    B. the colonies did not have the
       right to rule themselves.

    C. Northern colonial leaders
       could enforce any laws they
       chose to.

    D. all men are born with certain
       rights that the government
       cannot take away.

Below is the Fourth Amendment to the United States Constitution. Review it and answer the following question.

"The right of the people to be secure in their persons, houses, papers, and effects, against unreasonable searches and seizures, shall be violated, and no warrants shall issue, but upon probable cause, supported by Oath or affirmation, and particularly describing the place to be searched, and the persons or things to be seized."

69. Based on the Fourth Amendment, which of the following is **most** accurate? SS4H5

A. Citizens may not be searched without a warrant or probable cause.

B. Law enforcement officers may search a citizen's house anytime they choose.

C. Accused people who have the right to a lawyer.

D. A person who is found "not guilty" may not be charged with the same crime again.

70. What do Jacques Cartier and Samuel de Champlain have in common? SS4H2

A. They were French explorers.

B. They were Spanish explorers.

C. They discovered the Hudson River together.

D. They were descendants of Native Americans.

EVALUATION CHART FOR GEORGIA GRADE 4 CRCT IN SOCIAL STUDIES

Directions: On the following chart, circle the question numbers that you answered incorrectly and evaluate the results. These questions are based on the Georgia Competency Standards. Then turn to the appropriate topics (listed by chapters), read the explanations, and complete the exercises. Review other chapters as needed. Finally, complete the practice test(s) to assess your progress and further prepare you for the **Georgia Grade 4 Social Studies Test**.

Note: Some question numbers will appear under multiple chapters because those questions require demonstration of multiple skills.

Chapter	Diagnostic Test Question
1. Historical Understandings: Native American Peoples and Colonial America	1, 2, 3, 14, 15, 19, 27, 30, 34, 41, 44, 48, 49, 53, 58, 62, 66, 67, 70
2. The American Revolution	23, 39, 60, 68
3. The New Nation	9, 24, 40, 69
4. The United States: 1800 – 1861	8, 11, 25, 32, 42, 54, 55
5. Geographic Understandings	4, 10, 20, 26, 33, 38, 45, 52, 56, 61, 65
6. Government and Civics	7, 12, 16, 17, 18, 22, 28, 31, 35, 36, 46, 47, 51, 57, 63
7. Economic Understanding	6, 13, 21, 29, 37, 43, 50, 59, 64

Chapter 1
Historical Understandings:
Native American Peoples and
Colonial America

This chapter addresses the following GPS-based CRCT standard(s):

SS4H1	The student will describe how early Native American cultures developed in North America.
SS4H2	The student will describe European exploration in North America.
SS4H3	The student will explain the factors that shaped British colonial America.

1.1 THE FIRST AMERICANS

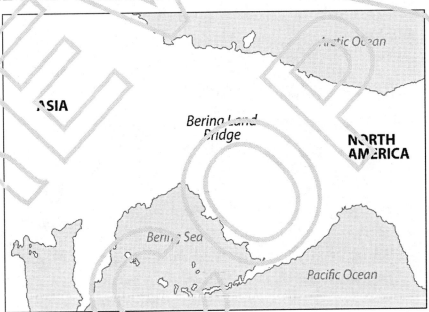

Bering Land Bridge

Historians are people who study history. Most historians believe that the first Americans migrated (moved) to North America from Asia. Today, North America and Asia are separated by water. Thousands of years ago, they were likely connected by ice. People living in Asia walked across this ice bridge to

North America. Over many centuries, they made their way to South America and other parts of the Western Hemisphere (western half of the world). Because they were the first people to live in the Americas, they became known as **Native Americans**.

DIFFERENT NATIVE AMERICAN PEOPLES

Early Native Americans

Different groups of Native Americans lived in North America. The **Inuit** settled in arctic regions that today form Greenland and northern Canada. The **Kwakiutl** settled in what became southwest Canada and the northwestern United States. The **Nez Perce** lived in the Columbus River Plateau. Historians believe that the Nez Perce lived for more than 10,000 years in parts of modern-day Washington, Idaho, and Oregon before the first US explorers arrived. The **Hopi** settled in what is now the US southwest. They built towns long before the first Europeans arrived in the region. The Midwest Plains became home to the **Pawnee**. In the region that became the southeastern United States, the **Seminoles** lived and thrived.

NATIVE AMERICAN CULTURES

Inuit Igloos

Native Americans relied on their **environment** for food, clothing, and shelter. The Inuit lived in cold, arctic regions. They relied on hunting and fishing. They hunted whales, walruses, seals,

Plains Teepees

caribou, and polar bears. The Inuit used the meat of these animals for food. The hides they often used for clothes, shelter, and kayaks (small, one-man boats). Native Americans in heavily forested regions used the wood of trees to build homes and provide what they needed. They ate many of the berries, nuts, and edible plants the forests provided. They also hunted and ate forest animals, using their furs and hides for clothing and shelter. Animal bones and stone served to make tools and weapons. Native Americans of the Great Plains relied heavily on the buffalo for what they needed. They ate buffalo meat and used buffalo hides for clothes and teepees (tent-like homes). Since they did not have much wood, they sometimes burned buffalo dung to build fires. Native Americans that lived along rivers and coastlines fished. The Hopi learned how to farm in the dry regions of the Southwest. People in other regions learned to grow crops suitable to their environment. Wherever they lived, Native Americans used their natural surroundings to survive. As a result, Native American cultures were very different. Native Americans in one part of North America did not live the same way or have the same customs as Native Americans in other parts.

Practice 1.1: The First Americans

1. The first Americans are known as
   A. Hopi.
   B. Seminoles.
   C. Pre-Americans.
   D. Native Americans

2. The Inuit lived in
   A. the Southwest.
   B. arctic regions.
   C. towns.
   D. Georgia.

3. Which of the following Native American peoples lived in what is today the northwest United States?
   A. Hopi and Seminoles
   B. Inuit and Pawnee
   C. Kwakiutl and Nez Perce
   D. Inuit and Seminoles

4. All Native Americans relied on which of the following to survive?
   A. fishing
   B. nuts and berries
   C. farming
   D. their environment

1.2 EUROPEAN EXPLORATION OF NORTH AMERICA

SPANISH EXPLORATION

Several European nations had colonies in North America. **Colonies** are settlements established by a country in a separate, foreign land. The Spanish were the first to successfully establish colonies in North America.

CHRISTOPHER COLUMBUS

Christopher Columbus

In 1492, **Christopher Columbus** led a voyage paid for by Spain. The purpose of the trip was to find a faster way to reach Asia so that Spain could trade with places like India and China.

Columbus Landing in Hispaniola

Columbus reached an island which he thought was just off the coast of Asia. It was really in the Bahamas. Columbus sent word back to Spain of the new land he'd found. On his second voyage, he established Spain's first permanent colony in the Americas: Hispaniola. Columbus claimed the territory for Spain even though Native Americans already lived there. Soon, more Spanish explorers came to the Americas. They were motivated by **God, gold**, and **glory**. Some came as missionaries to spread Catholicism to the Native Americans. Others came to find wealth in the form of land, gold, and other natural resources. Still others wanted to become famous and win honor as great adventurers.

PONCE DE LEON, BALBOA, AND DE SOTO

Ponce de Leon Exploring Florida

Juan Ponce de Leon heard stories of an American spring that had great power. Anyone who drank from it would become young again. He went to the New World, in part, to find the *Fountain of Youth*. He never found the spring. However, while searching for it in 1513, he discovered the territory known as Florida.

Vasco Nunez Balboa landed on the Atlantic coast of the Isthmus of Panama. The Isthmus of Panama is a narrow strip of land that connects North America and South America. In 1513, Balboa led a group of Spaniards and Native Americans on a journey across the isthmus. He and his fellow Spaniards became the first Europeans to reach the Pacific coast of the Americas.

Balboa Reaching the Pacific Coast

In 1539, **Hernando de Soto** landed in North America. He was the first known European to explore the territory of Georgia. De Soto hoped to gain glory and find lots of gold. De Soto's expedition failed. He died somewhere along the Mississippi River in 1542, never having found his abundant gold. Spain eventually established settlements in parts of what became the US South and Southwest.

FRENCH EXPLORATION

Jacques Cartier was one of the earliest French explorers. He made several voyages to what is today Canada. He explored the St. Lawrence River, but failed to establish a permanent colony. Later, **Samuel de Champlain** established France's first successful colony in 1608 at Quebec. Unlike the English who established colonies along the Atlantic

French Fur Trade

coast (see section 1.3), the French used rivers and inland waterways to control areas further inland. North America's abundant forests and wildlife allowed France to make a lot of money from its **fur trade**. French traders would get fur by trapping deer, beaver, or other animals, or by trading with Native Americans. Then, they would sell their furs and hides to traders who sold them in Europe. Native Americans and French traders relied on one another for commerce.

ENGLISH EXPLORATION

John Cabot

John Cabot was the first known explorer to reach North America on behalf of England. He reached Canada in 1497. However, when he failed to return from his second voyage, England did not sponsor another journey to America for many years. **Henry Hudson** explored for both the English and the Dutch. In 1609, he discovered the Hudson River in what is today New York. At first, he thought he had found a water route to the Pacific Ocean. He turned back, however, when he realized that he had not.

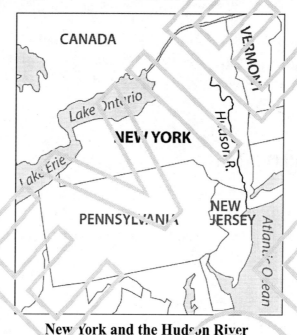

New York and the Hudson River

EUROPEAN EXPLORATION'S EFFECTS ON NATIVE AMERICANS

Some encounters between **Europeans and Native Americans** were peaceful. Others were violent. Christopher Columbus killed and enslaved many of the Native Americans he encountered in Hispaniola, even though they welcomed him peacefully when he first arrived. Columbus forced them to search for gold and other valuable resources that he could ship back to Spain. Hernando de Soto traded with some of the Native Americans he encountered. He conquered and killed others. Although the Spaniards were often outnumbered, they had more advanced weapons, like guns and crossbows. The Spanish also brought with them deadly diseases like smallpox, measles, and influenza. Native Americans had never been exposed to these diseases. Their immune systems had no resistance, and many of them died.

Since French settlers tended to rely on good relations with Native Americans for their fur trade, they often had more peaceful relations. For the most part, the French did not try to establish large, permanent settlements. Early French colonists usually planned to live in North America only long enough to gain wealth before returning to Europe. Native Americans did not view the French to be as big a threat as English settlers who came to the New World to live permanently and claim large areas of land. (We will discuss English colonists relations with Native Americans more in section 1.3)

Practice 1.2: European Exploration of North America

1. When a country establishes a settlement in a foreign land, that settlement is called

   A. an exploration.

   B. a colony.

   C. a journey.

   D. a trading post.

2. Juan Ponce de Leon and Vasco Nunez Balboa were both

   A. Spanish explorers.

   B. Spanish fur traders.

   C. French explorers.

   D. Native American leaders who interacted with Europeans.

3. Christopher Columbus' treatment of Native Americans can **best** be described as

   A. friendly.

   B. violent and hostile.

   C. peaceful but not friendly.

   D. fair.

1.3 THE BRITISH COLONIES

SOUTHERN, MIDDLE, AND NEW ENGLAND COLONIES

British colonists came for many reasons. Some came for **economic reasons**. They heard that North America offered land and resources. They traveled to the New World because it offered more money than they could make in England. Others came for **religious reasons**. They did not agree with the Church of England and wanted to escape religious persecution. They sailed for North America to found religious communities based on their own beliefs. Some had **political reasons**. They wanted to escape political persecution and govern themselves.

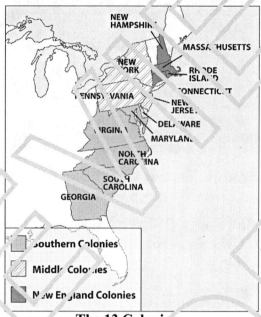

The 13 Colonies

Historians usually divide the British colonies into three regions. The **New England Colonies** included Massachusetts, New Hampshire, Rhode Island, and Connecticut. The **Middle Colonies** were New York, New Jersey, Pennsylvania, and Delaware. The **Southern Colonies** were made up of Maryland, Virginia, North Carolina, South Carolina, and Georgia. Some colonies were **royal colonies**. They were governed directly by the king through a royal governor. Other colonies were proprietary or charter colonies. **Proprietary colonies** were colonies granted to a group of private owners for development. These owners' main focus was to make money. **Charter colonies** were colonies formed by a group of trustees. Trustees were officials entrusted with taking care of the colony. Some trustees might live in the colony. Others might remain in England. The king granted the trustees a charter to establish the colony and set up a government. The colony of

Georgia was first established as a charter colony. Its founders wanted it to be a place for English debtors (people imprisoned in England for failing to pay their debts). The British government wanted it to serve as a buffer between British colonies to the north and the Spanish colony of Florida to the South. Georgia later became a royal colony during the 1750s.

THE SOUTHERN COLONIES

JAMESTOWN

John Rolfe

In 1607, England established its first successful colony at **Jamestown**, Virginia. It was founded by the Virginia Company. The Virginia Company hoped to make money off of

Colonial Jamestown

the raw materials the colony would provide. The first few years, however, were hard. Bitter cold winters, disease, and starvation killed many of the settlers. Fortunately, the local Native Americans helped the colonists and provided food. The colony was saved when a man named John Rolfe discovered a new crop: tobacco! Tobacco became very popular and made many land owners in Virginia wealthy. To attract laborers to help grow more tobacco, Virginia promised fifty acres of land to those who would settle in the colony.

THE SOUTHERN ECONOMY

Tobacco became an important cash crop for Virginia, Maryland, and North Carolina. A **cash crop** is a crop that provides a region with a large amount of its income. The hot and wet climates of South Carolina and Georgia made rice and indigo important cash crops further south. Southern colonies also produced tar, pitch, and turpentine from the abundant forests that existed in the region.

The South's reliance on cash crops led to the rise of the **plantation system**. Plantations were huge farms owned by wealthy landowners. Plantations required lots of manual labor. Indentured servants and slaves became important parts of the southern economy. **Indentured servants** were people who could not afford to come to North America on their own. They

Early Plantation

agreed to work for a landowner for up to seven years in exchange for the landowner paying for their trip. After their service was up, indentured servants became small land owners. Many indentured servants suffered harsh treatment by their masters once they arrived in the New World.

As available land decreased, many large landowners decided to use slaves instead of indentured servants. **Slavery** was a system in which people were "owned" as property. Since slaves usually didn't gain their freedom, they were not entitled to land once a period of service was up. By the mid-1600s, slavery existed throughout the colonies. At first, Native Americans were sometimes made slaves. However, Native Americans knew the land and had family and friends to help them if they escaped. Europeans realized that it was easier to use black slaves shipped from Africa.

Large plantations tended to lie along rivers and inland water ways. Plantation owners often had direct access to shipping without having to transport their products to major ports. As a result, the South did not develop the major centers of commerce and large cities that arose in the North.

SOUTHERN SOCIETY

Southern Landowner

Southern society was made up of rich plantation owners, poor farmers, a few merchants and artisans (craftsmen), and slaves. Most southerners accepted the idea that the wealthy, upper class was superior to the lower, poorer classes. People believed that upper-class men should be the ones in positions of leadership and authority.

Public education did not exist in the Southern Colonies. Any schooling that occurred among poorer southerners took place in the home. Wealthy southerners often hired private tutors or sent their children to Europe to be educated. The Southern Colonies were established mostly for economic reasons rather than religious (Maryland, which was started as a colony for Catholics, was the one exception). For this reason, rich landowners usually remained part of the Church of England (Anglican Church) because it was better for them politically and economically. Over time, Methodist and Baptist faiths became common among poorer southerners and settlers along the frontier. These churches grew because they used new methods to reach rural areas.

Colonial Puritans

THE NEW ENGLAND COLONIES

THE PURITANS

The **Puritans** settled in New England for religious reasons. They did not agree with the Church of England. They wanted to establish a community based on their own understanding of the Bible rather than Anglican traditions. In 1620, a group of Puritans established a colony at **Plymouth**, Massachusetts. These Puritans became known as the **Pilgrims**. They had a hard time adjusting to life in New England. But Native Americans helped them and taught them how to grow crops in order to survive. The Pilgrims and some of their Native American neighbors celebrated the first

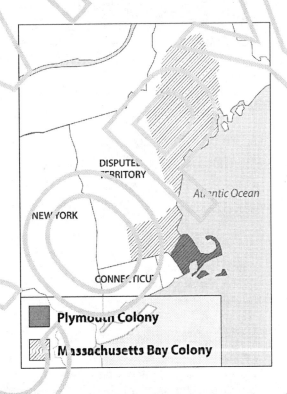

Thanksgiving in 1621. Later, another group of Puritans settled further north and established the **Massachusetts Bay Colony**.

Not all New Englanders agreed with everything the Puritan leaders taught. Roger Williams and Anne Hutchinson left Massachusetts over religious differences. They helped form the colony of Rhode Island. Other Puritan settlers founded Connecticut and New Hampshire.

NEW ENGLAND'S ECONOMY

Rather than raising cash crops, the New England Colonies relied heavily on the Atlantic Ocean. Shipbuilding, trade, and fishing became leading industries. Boston, Massachusetts, became a booming city due to shipping and commerce. Although New Englanders grew crops, their farms tended to be smaller. Most farmers raised only enough to support their families.

NEW ENGLAND SOCIETY

New England Church

The Puritan church was very important in New England. In Massachusetts, every settler had to attend and support the Puritan church. Dissenters (people who disagreed with the church) often had to leave the colony. The Puritans had a strong sense of faith, family, and community. They were the first English settlers to promote public education. Puritans believed that everyone should be familiar with the Bible. Therefore, they wanted people to learn how to read. Most boys and a few girls attended schools. Colonists in New England also founded two of the nation's earliest colleges: Harvard and Yale. The purpose of these colleges was to train ministers.

THE MIDDLE COLONIES

Colonial New York

The Middle Colonies were in between New England and the Southern Colonies. Other nations, such as Sweden and the Netherlands, had colonies in the region before the British arrived. Much of the Middle Colonies offered religious freedom. The region was also home to large cities like New York and

Philadelphia. People from all walks of life lived and worked in these cities. The Middle Colonies were more diverse (had more types of people) than any other part of the British colonies.

ECONOMY OF THE MIDDLE COLONIES

The Middle Colonies depended on both farming and commerce. Farmers raised crops like wheat, barley, and rye. Cities were home to businesses and often served as important ports for shipping products overseas. Because the region did not rely solely on cash crops, there were not as many slaves in the Middle Colonies as in the South. Slaves in the Middle Colonies often worked in shops and cities, as well as on farms. Thanks to inland waterways, the Middle Colonies also benefited from a thriving fur trade. Many colonists in this region had good relations with Native Americans.

SOCIETY IN THE MIDDLE COLONIES

William Penn

Under the leadership of William Penn, Pennsylvania became a homeland for **Quakers**. This religious group did not believe the upper class was better than the lower class. Quakers also believed in equality for women, pacifism (non-violence), and treating Native Americans fairly. They made Pennsylvania a place of religious tolerance. This attracted other religious groups to the region. German Lutherans, Scotch-Irish Presbyterians, and Swiss Mennonites all settled in Pennsylvania.

Because New York was first a Dutch colony, its residents spoke different languages and practiced different customs. It also featured different religions. Jews, as well as Christians, settled in New York. The city became home to the colonies' first synagogue (place of Jewish worship). The freedom found in the Middle Colonies made the region popular. People who felt

Quakers

persecuted in the South or New England often moved to the Middle Colonies. Meanwhile, as cities continued to grow, a class order developed. Merchants who dealt in foreign trade formed the upper class. Sailors and unskilled workers made up the lower classes. The middle class included artisans, retailers, and businessmen.

COLONIAL GOVERNMENT

Because the colonies were very far from England, British leaders had to trust the colonists to govern themselves. England adopted a policy called **salutary neglect**. The policy let the colonies handle much of their own government, so long as they remained loyal to England. The colonies established **representative governments**, in which the people elected their own leaders. Colonial governors appointed by the king were supposed to be in charge. But colonial legislatures made up of locally elected leaders had most of the power. Elected members of the legislatures were more popular and controlled much of the money.

House of Burgesses

Governors and legislators often did not get along. The governor represented the king. The legislators represented the people of the colony.

The first legislative body in the New World was Virginia's **House of Burgesses** in 1619. Although only white males who owned property could vote, this body demonstrated a belief that citizens should have a voice in their government.

Town Meeting in New England

In New England, representative government took the form of **town meetings**. Local citizens met together to discuss and vote on issues. Once again, it gave citizens a say in their government. Puritan leaders, however, still believed that government should seek to enforce the will of God rather than satisfy the will of the people. For this reason, power tended to rest in the hands of church leaders who told colonists how to live. Tensions sometimes arose between church leaders and people who disagreed. Eventually, legislative bodies formed in cities like Boston.

Colonists believed strongly in representative government. The feeling that Britain was trying to deny colonists this right was one of the main reasons colonists declared independence from Great Britain in 1776.

WOMEN, BLACKS, AND NATIVE AMERICANS DURING THE BRITISH COLONIAL PERIOD

COLONIAL WOMEN

In most cases, **colonial women** were considered less important than men. They could not vote, nor could they usually attend school. By law, they were considered to be under their husband's or father's control. Their main responsibilities were raising children and taking care of the home. In some cases, when a husband or father was gone or had died, women owned property or had more responsibility. Sometimes, women would run a plantation or business when fathers or husbands

Colonial Women

were away. Since there were fewer workers in the colonies than in Europe, women sometimes filled roles in the New World that would have only been open to men in England. Some colonial women worked as shopkeepers, tavern hostesses, or even doctors.

BLACKS IN THE COLONIES

Colonial Slaves

The first Africans in the English colonies arrived in 1619 at Jamestown, Virginia. Some were slaves. Others were indentured servants. Indentured servants gained their freedom after a set number of years. Some slaves managed to save money and buy their freedom. Free blacks sometimes owned land and became masters of indentured servants and African slaves themselves. In time, however, economic concerns and racism made it harder for black slaves to gain freedom or for free blacks to exercise the same rights as whites.

In South Carolina and Georgia, where rice was the main crop, African American slaves worked mostly in the fields. They remained largely separated from white society and did not adopt as many white customs as slaves in other regions. Since growing tobacco took less time than rice, slaves in Virginia, North Carolina, and Maryland had more contact with whites. They adopted more European customs and behavior. In the Middle Colonies and New England, slaves were often trained in a craft and then put to work in shops and cities. Some were even allowed to make money and buy their own freedom.

Colonial Slave Working

Slavery was a horrible institution. Slaves were bought and sold like property. Slave families were often separated. Young children were taken from parents. Husbands and wives were sold away from each other. Masters forced slaves to work hard for long periods of time. Slaves who did not work hard enough or tried to escape usually suffered beatings and abuse.

NATIVE AMERICANS AND COLONISTS

At times, Native Americans and British colonists got along peacefully. It is likely that the colonies at Jamestown and Plymouth would not have survived their first winters had Native Americans not given them food. At other times, however, relations were not good. British settlers often looked down on the Native Americans. Native Americans valued leisure time and were not interested in working for the colonists. This led many settlers to view them as lazy and weak. From time to time, violence broke out. In March 1622, Native Americans launched a surprise attack on Jamestown that killed 300 colonists. Residents of Jamestown struck back, killing at least as many Native Americans. In 1644, Native Americans attacked Jamestown again. Their attack failed and their chief was shot and killed. From then on, the European settlers had control of the colony. But conflicts with Native Americans in the western regions of Virginia continued for several more decades. As land became scarce, white settlers moved west and fought Native Americans for land along the Virginia frontier.

King Philip's War

At first, relations between colonial settlers and Native Americans in New England were peaceful. Eventually, however, settlers moved west. They pushed Native Americans off their lands. This led to violence. In 1675, a Native American leader known as King Philip (his Native American name was Metacom) united Native Americans in New England in a war against English settlers. Despite killing nearly 2,000 colonists, Metacom's forces had to retreat when the settlers struck back. King Philip's War ended when colonial soldiers cornered Metacom in a Rhode Island cave and shot him through the heart.

White colonists continued moving west. Tensions between Native Americans who already lived in western territories and British colonists increased. Native Americans suffered as they lost more and more territory to whites. Many Native Americans allied with French colonists who also opposed the British. Eventually, such tensions led to a war between France and Great Britain for control of North America.

Practice 1.3: The British Colonies

1. The first English colony in North America was

   A. Plymouth.

   B. Georgia.

   C. Massachusetts.

   D. Jamestown.

2. Historians divide the British colonies into which of the following three categories?

   A. Royal, Representative, Colonial

   B. Southern, Northern, Western

   C. New England, Middle, Southern

   D. Charter, Jamestown, Puritan

3. Where would one probably have found the **most** diversity in 1660?

   A. Jamestown

   B. Plymouth

   C. Boston

   D. New York

4. King Philip's War was an example of

   A. the evils of slavery.

   B. how easily indentured servants got angry at their masters.

   C. Britain's decision to push the Spanish out of Georgia.

   D. the tension that existed between colorists and Native Americans.

CHAPTER 1 REVIEW

Key Terms, People, and Concepts

historians

Native Americans

Inuit

Kwakiutl

Nez Perce

Hopi

Pawnee

Seminoles

Native Americans' dependence on the environment

colonies

Christopher Columbus

God, gold, and glory

Juan Ponce de León

Vasco Nunez Balboa

Hernando de Soto

Jacques Cartier

Samuel de Champlain

fur trade

John Cabot

Henry Hudson

relations between Europeans and Native Americans

economic, religious, and political reasons English settlers came to North America

New England Colonies

Middle Colonies

Southern Colonies

royal colonies

proprietary colonies

charter colonies

Jamestown

cash crop

plantation system

indentured servants

slavery

southern society

Puritans

Plymouth

Pilgrims

Massachusetts Bay Colony

New England's economy

New England society

Middle Colonies' economy

Middle Colony society

Quakers

salutary neglect

representative government

House of Burgesses

town meetings

colonial women

colonial blacks

Native Americans during the colonial period

Multiple Choice Questions

1. The Inuit, Nez Perce, and Hopi are all considered Native Americans because they

   A. established the first colonies in North America.

   B. were the first Europeans in North America.

   C. descend from the first people to live in North America.

   D. learned to rely on their environment for food.

2. The natural environment was very important to early Native Americans because it

   A. allowed them to raise cash crops.

   B. provided food and shelter.

   C. prevented Europeans from taking all their land.

   D. allowed them to learn farming and fur trading from Europeans.

Look at the map below and answer question #3.

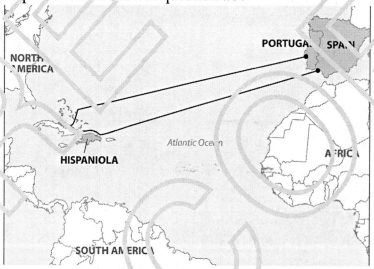

3. Whose journey is shown on the map above?

   A. Christopher Columbus   C. John Cabot

   B. Juan Ponce de Leon   D. Henry Hudson

Look at the map below and answer questions #4 and #5.

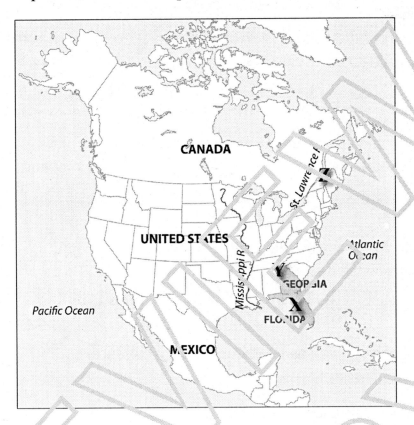

4. Who explored the area marked 'Z'?

   A. Juan Ponce de Leon

   B. Jacques Cartier

   C. Hernando de Soto

   D. John Cabot

5. In which region on the map did Juan Ponce de Leon **most likely** meet Seminoles?

   A. X

   B. Y

   C. Z

   D. Seminoles did not live in the region Ponce de Leon explored.

6. Manuel is a Spanish soldier. In 1513, he and a group of his fellow adventurers become the first Europeans ever to see the Pacific Ocean from the coast of the Americas. Who is the leader of Manuel's group?
   A. Christopher Columbus
   B. Jacques Cartier
   C. Vasco Nunez Balboa
   D. Hernando de Soto

7. Which colonial region relied **mostly** on cash crops?
   A. Southern
   B. Middle
   C. New England
   D. none of the above

8. Most blacks who lived in the British colonies were
   A. indentured servants.
   B. Native Americans.
   C. Puritans.
   D. slaves.

9. Which region was most impacted by the Puritans?
   A. Southern Colonies
   B. New York and Philadelphia
   C. Middle Colonies
   D. New England

10. Colonial women
   A. often served in colonial government
   B. were not allowed to vote.
   C. usually ran the family business or plantation.
   D. were rarely responsible for the home.

11. Describe in three or four sentences how Native Americans were treated during the colonial period by the Spanish, French, and British.

Chapter 2
The American Revolution

This chapter addresses the following GPS-based CRCT standard(s):

SS4H4	The student will explain the causes, events, and results of the American Revolution.

2.1 CAUSES OF THE REVOLUTION

FRENCH AND INDIAN WAR

In the 1750s, Great Britain and France were the two most powerful nations in North America. In 1754, the two countries began fighting each other in the **French and Indian War**. During the war, British colonists and troops fought against the French and their Native American allies. In 1763, France finally surrendered. After the war, Great Britain owned all land east of the Mississippi River.

French and Indian War

TENSIONS RISE BETWEEN GREAT BRITAIN AND THE COLONIES

BRITISH IMPERIAL POLICY

Enforcing Laws

Soon after the French and Indian War, the colonies and Great Britain began to have problems. The colonists were used to governing themselves. They did not like **Britain's Imperial Policy**. Britain used its power to try to control the colonies. The British government believed that the colonists should help pay for the French and Indian War. As a result, they passed laws meant to make the colonists pay their share. These laws offended the colonists.

THE STAMP ACT

One of the laws that made colonists angry was the **Stamp Act** of 1765. The Stamp Act placed a tax on all legal documents, licenses, newspapers, and so on. All documents had to have a government stamp. Before colonists could get the stamp, they had to pay the tax. Many colonists hated the Stamp Act. One colonial leader, James Otis of Massachusetts, proclaimed, **"No taxation without representation!"** In other words, the colonists believed they should not have to pay taxes since they had no one representing them in Parliament (the lawmaking body of Britain's government). Protests against the Stamp Act spread. Many colonists became patriots. Patriots opposed Great Britain's policies and eventually called for

The Stamp Act of 1765

independence for the colonies. Others colonists were loyalists. Loyalists were colonists who remained loyal to the king and wanted to remain part of Great Britain.

THE SONS OF LIBERTY

The Sons of Liberty

A number of patriots called for boycotts. Boycotts were protests in which people refused to buy British products. Colonists hoped that British businesses would get tired of losing money and pressure Parliament to change the law. Patriot groups like the **Sons of Liberty** formed in several colonies. The Sons of Liberty protested laws like the Stamp Act. They used violence and threats to make sure that no stamps were sold and everyone stuck to the boycotts.

BOSTON TEA PARTY

After the Stamp Act Parliament passed the Tea Act in 1773. It stated that Britain's East India Company could sell tea in the colonies without paying the normal tax. This allowed the company to sell tea for less money. Patriots saw this as a trick to get the colonies to buy British tea. They called for more boycotts. In December 1773 Boston patriots dressed as

The Boston Tea Party

Native Americans and marched to Boston Harbor. They raided ships hauling British tea and threw the crates overboard. This event became known as the **Boston Tea Party**. Afterwards, Parliament passed the Intolerable Acts. These acts closed Boston Harbor and placed a military governor over Massachusetts. Anger over the Intolerable Acts helped spark the American Revolution.

LEXINGTON AND CONCORD

Lexington and Concord

Fighting finally broke out in April 1775 at **Lexington and Concord**. As British troops made their way to seize weapons stored at Concord, Massachusetts, they were met at Lexington by colonial militia (voluntary, local military units made up of private citizens rather than full-time soldiers). It was there that someone fired the shot that started the American Revolution.

INDEPENDENCE DECLARED

In June 1776, the Second Continental Congress decided to declare independence from Great Britain. The Continental Congress was made up of delegates (representatives) from the thirteen colonies. During the American Revolution, it became

Signing the Declaration of Independence

the United States' governing body. One of the delegates, Thomas Jefferson, wrote the **Declaration of Independence**. It stated that men are born with certain rights that the government cannot take away. These rights include "life, liberty, and the pursuit of happiness." The Declaration claimed that Great Britain had abused its power and had not ruled properly. It declared that the colonies had a right to rule themselves! On July 4, 1776, the delegates signed and adopted the declaration.

Practice 2.1: Causes of the Revolution

1. The Stamp Act upset colonists because it was

   A. a tax the colonists found unfair.

   B. a harsh law passed after the Boston Tea Party.

   C. part of British boycotts against American goods.

   D. meant to lower the price of British tea.

2. In December 1773, patriots dressed as Native Americans raided British ships and threw crates overboard. This event is known as the

   A. British Imperial Policy.   C. Battle of Lexington.

   B. Boston Tea Party.   D. French and Indian War.

3. What is the passage below **most likely** referring to?

Men are born with certain rights that the government can not take away. These rights include "life, liberty, and the pursuit of happiness."

   A. British Imperial Policy

   B. the Declaration of Independence

   C. Sons of Liberty

   D. the meeting at Concord

2.2 THE AMERICAN REVOLUTION

KEY FIGURES OF THE AMERICAN REVOLUTION

Below is a list of some of the most important people during the American Revolution.

King George III

George Washington

King George III was the king of England during the American Revolutionary War.

George Washington was a Virginia landowner who had fought for the British during the French and Indian War. The Continental Congress chose Washington to lead America's Continental Army during the Revolution. Washington overcame many challenges to lead the Continental Army to victory. He later led the Constitutional Convention and was elected to serve as the United States' first president. He is often called the "father of the country" because of his role in winning independence and establishing the government.

Benjamin Franklin was a respected inventor, scientist, and writer. He served as the colonies' ambassador (representative) to Great Britain before the revolution. At first, he wanted peace between the colonies and Britain. However, he eventually supported independence and the revolution. During the revolution, Franklin went to Paris and convinced France to help America win its independence.

Benjamin Franklin

John Adams

John Adams was a lawyer who supported independence. He represented Massachusetts in the First and Second Continental Congress. He was also the one to nominate George Washington to be commander of the American army. He helped Thomas Jefferson draft the Declaration of Independence. For much of the war, he served as an ambassador to Europe. He later became the United States' first vice president and its second president.

Thomas Jefferson was a young delegate to the Second Continental Congress. He wrote most of the Declaration of Independence in 1776. During the war he served for two years as the governor of Virginia. After the revolution he served as the United States' ambassador to France. He eventually served as the First Secretary of state and won election as the third president of the United States.

Thomas Jefferson

Benedict Arnold

Benedict Arnold was an American soldier and a talented commander. He led the American victory at Saratoga, but grew angry after the credit was given to General Horatio Gates. Arnold later betrayed the revolution and tried to give the British secret information. His plan failed and Arnold barely escaped.

Patrick Henry was a radical supporter of independence. He is most famous for a speech he gave before the Virginia legislature on March 23, 1775. Henry convinced Virginia to support independence with his fiery words: "give me liberty, or give me death!" Although historians debate whether or not Henry said these exact words, he definitely helped convince Virginia to support the revolution.

Patrick Henry

THE FIRST YEAR OF THE REVOLUTION

By the summer of 1776, colonists and British forces had been fighting for over a year. King George III of England did not expect a long war. After all, the British had one of the world's most powerful armies and its strongest navy. How could a bunch of untrained colonists possibly defeat them? The colonists, however, were fighting for their homeland and the right to govern themselves. They were more determined to win the war.

IMPORTANT BATTLES

TRENTON AND PRINCETON

Washington Crossing the Delaware

In March 1776, the British marched to New York and forced General Washington's army to retreat. The Colonial army was close to losing the revolution. Then, on Christmas night in 1776, Washington's forces crossed the Delaware River and surprised the enemy at **Trenton,** New Jersey. Then Washington launched another surprise attack at **Princeton.** Washington's victories in New Jersey gave America hope that it could win the revolution.

SARATOGA

In September 1777, the United States won a key victory at **Saratoga,** New York. Saratoga was very important because it convinced the French that the colonies could win the war. France finally decided to give money and military support to help defeat the British.

Battle of Saratoga

YORKTOWN

General Washington

After a bloody battle in North Carolina, British General Lord Cornwallis marched north to the coastal town of Yorktown, Virginia. He hoped to receive help and supplies from British ships. Realizing that Cornwallis was trapped on the Virginia peninsula, General Washington marched south to face him. He wanted to pin Cornwallis between the Continental Army and the Atlantic Ocean. Meanwhile, the French navy kept British ships from coming to Cornwallis's rescue. On October 19, 1781, Cornwallis surrendered to Washington at **Yorktown**. It was the last major battle of the war. The Americans and British finally signed the Treaty of Paris in 1783. The treaty ended the war, and Great Britain officially recognized the United States as an independent nation.

Practice 2 2: The American Revolution

1. Who led the Continental Army and later became the first president of the United States?
   A. George Washington
   B. John Adams
   C. Benedict Arnold
   D. Patrick Henry

2. Benedict Arnold is most remembered as a traitor, but he was also a great commander who won a key victory for the Americans at
   A. Yorktown.
   B. Lexington.
   C. Princeton.
   D. Saratoga.

3. Which battle ended the American Revolution?
   A. Lexington
   B. Yorktown
   C. Saratoga
   D. Concord

CHAPTER 2 REVIEW

Key Terms, People, and Concepts

French and Indian War   Saratoga
Britain's Imperial Policy   Yorktown
Stamp Act   King George III
"No taxation without representation"   George Washington
Sons of Liberty   Benjamin Franklin
Boston Tea Party   John Adams
Lexington and Concord   Thomas Jefferson
Declaration of Independence   Benedict Arnold
Trenton and Princeton   Patrick Henry

Multiple Choice Questions

1. Which of the following **most directly** led to the saying, "no taxation without representation?"

    A. the Stamp Act   C. a loyalist meeting in Concord

    B. Native American boycotts   D. the Boston Tea Party

2. The Sons of Liberty

    A. forced colonists to pay taxes on British goods.

    B. formed an alliance with Native Americans.

    C. used violence and threats to support boycotts of British goods.

    D. organized meetings in support of Great Britain.

3. What is the passage below most likely referring to?

> We, the Representatives of the United States of America, declare that these united colonies should be free and independent states. They are cleared of allegiance to Great Britain and have the right to rule themselves.

    A. the Stamp Act

    B. the Declaration of Independence

    C. Speech at Lexington

    D. the Boston Tea Party

4. The Boston Tea Party

    A. was led by colonial loyalists.

    B. led to the Stamp Act of 1765.

    C. happened because of the high cost of tea.

    D. was a protest against British policies.

5. Most of the Declaration of Independence was written by

    A. Thomas Jefferson.

    B. George Washington.

    C. Benjamin Franklin.

    D. John Adams.

6. Who is the list below referring to?

- a patriot
- nominated Washington to command the Continental Army
- became the United States' first vice president and its second president

    A. Thomas Jefferson

    B. John Adams

    C. Benjamin Franklin

    D. Benedict Arnold

7. During the American Revolution, which battle led to France deciding to help the Americans?

   A. Trenton

   B. Yorktown

   C. Saratoga

   D. Concord

8. In April 1775, as British troops made their way to seize weapons at Concord, they were met by colonial militia at

   A. Yorktown

   B. Boston

   C. Lexington

   D. Saratoga

Chapter 3
The New Nation

This chapter addresses the following GPS-based CRCT standard(s):

| SS4H5 | The student will analyze the challenges faced by the new nation. |

3.1 FRAMING THE CONSTITUTION

ARTICLES OF CONFEDERATION AND THE NEED FOR CHANGE

The new nation ratified (accepted) its first set of national laws in 1781. It was called the **Articles of Confederation**. Unfortunately, the Articles of Confederation failed. It did not give enough power to the national government. It required at least nine of the thirteen states to agree before a new law could pass. Such agreement was rare. Also, the national government had no authority to tax citizens. This made it very difficult to raise money. It was hard to fund an army or carry out government duties. The national government had to rely on the willingness of the states to cooperate. If the states did not want to contribute money or support, then there was little the national government could do. By 1787, most agreed that change was necessary.

THE CONSTITUTIONAL CONVENTION

Constitutional Convention

In 1787, representatives from twelve states (only Rhode Island did not send a representative) met in Philadelphia. They wanted to revise (change in hopes of improving) the Articles of Confederation. After gathering, however, they decided to write a new set of laws. The document they came up with was the **United States Constitution**. Their gathering in Philadelphia became known as the **Constitutional Convention**. (See chapter 6, sections 6.1 and 6.2, for more regarding the powers of government under the Constitution.)

MAJOR LEADERS OF THE CONSTITUTIONAL CONVENTION

George Washington

Ben Franklin

Several leaders of the American Revolution also played key roles in the Constitutional Convention. **George Washington** presided over the convention. He eventually became the nation's first president. **Benjamin Franklin** served as the convention's elder statesmen. At eighty years of age, he rarely engaged in debate. His wisdom, however, proved valuable in helping the younger leaders to draft the Constitution.

James Madison

James Madison is often called the "Father of the Constitution." Madison was a young representative from Virginia. He was only thirty-six years old when he arrived at the Constitutional Convention. Madison had long believed that the United States needed a stronger national government. By the time leaders opened the convention, Madison had already come up with a plan. Many of the ideas he introduced, such as three branches of government and a bicameral (two-house) legislature, became part of the Constitution.

DEBATES AND COMPROMISE AT THE CONVENTION

The Original 13 States

The leaders at the Constitutional Convention did not always agree. Representatives wanted to make sure that the new set of laws did not hurt the interests of their home states. To settle these disagreements, leaders agreed to several **compromises**. A compromise is an agreement reached after both sides give something up. Neither side gets everything they want, but both sides get enough to be satisfied with the final decision. The **Great Compromise** settled the issue of representation. Everyone at the Constitutional Convention agreed that the new government should represent the people. They disagreed, however, over how to represent them. Larger states wanted a legislature made up of two houses. Each house would be based on population. States with the most people would have the most representatives. Smaller states hated this idea. They felt that it would not give them a fair voice in the national government. They favored having a legislature that had one house and gave each state an equal number of votes. The Great Compromise was a plan that combined these ideas. It set up a two-house legislature. One house, called the House of Representatives, is based on population. Larger states have more representatives. The second house, called the Senate, has two senators from each state. Smaller states are equally represented.

Slaves in the Late 1700s

Slavery was another big issue. Northern states had fewer slaves. Some even planned to emancipate (free) their slaves. They did not want to count slaves as part of the population. Southern states, however, had a lot of slaves. They wanted slaves to count as part of the population. The issue was important because population would affect a state's representation in Congress. The **Three-fifths Compromise** settled the dispute. It stated that each slave would count as three-fifths of a person.

Debate also surrounded the Atlantic slave trade (business of selling African slaves to slave owners in America). Northern states wanted to end the slave trade because their economy did not depend on slavery. Many

Slave Trade in the Late 1700s

northerners saw slavery as immoral as well. They felt slavery went against the principles of the Declaration of Independence. States in the Upper South (Virginia and Maryland) also wanted to end the slave trade. They already had a large number of slaves. The Upper South did not have enough land to support a huge slave population. Some also feared a slave rebellion. Leaders in the Upper South believed that ending the Atlantic slave trade would mean a profitable domestic slave trade for them. (Domestic slave trade means that they wanted to sell slaves from the Upper South to slave owners in the Lower South. If southern slave owners could no longer buy slaves from Africa, they would have to buy them from places like Virginia and Maryland.) Representatives from the Lower South (South Carolina and Georgia) wanted to keep the slave trade. They relied on cash crops and needed the slaves for labor. The **Slave Trade Compromise** allowed the Atlantic slave trade to continue for twenty years before Congress ended it.

Another big issue was the rights of states. Many feared a strong national government. They did not want a central government telling them what to do. Some states refused to ratify (accept) the Constitution until amendments were added limiting the government's power. One of these amendments (the **Tenth Amendment**) guarantees that certain powers are reserved for the states.

THE GOVERNMENT ESTABLISHED BY THE CONSTITUTION

SEPARATION OF POWERS

The representatives to the Constitutional Convention formed a government that included a **separation of powers**. Instead of giving all the governing authority to one leader or body, the Constitution establishes three branches of government.

Branches of Government

 Judicial

 Executive

 Legislative

THE LEGISLATIVE BRANCH: CONGRESS

The **legislative branch** makes the country's laws. Two houses make up the legislative branch. The **House of Representatives** includes representatives from each state. How many representatives each state has depends on population. States are divided into voting districts. The citizens of each district elect one person to represent them in the House of Representatives.

The Capitol Building

Representatives serve two-year terms. The **Senate** is made up of two senators from each state. Senators serve six-year terms. When the states first ratified the Constitution, state legislatures chose each state's senators. Today, however, citizens directly elect their senators. Both the House and the Senate must pass a bill (proposed law) before it can become a national law. Together, these two houses form **Congress**.

THE EXECUTIVE BRANCH: PRESIDENT, VICE PRESIDENT, AND THE PRESIDENT'S CABINET

President George Washington

The **executive branch** enforces the nation's laws. The **president of the United States** is the country's chief executive. He or she serves as the nation's leader The president commands the US military. He or she is also the country's chief representative when dealing with foreign nations. The **vice president** is the nation's second highest official. He or she presides over the US Senate. The vice president is also the next in line to become president if the president dies or cannot complete his or her four-year term in office.

A body called the **Electoral College** elects both the president and the vice president. The Electoral College is made up of delegates from each state. The number of delegates a state has is equal to its number of representatives and senators in Congress. Whichever candidate for president and vice president wins the most votes in the Electoral College wins the election.

Thomas Jefferson   Alexander Hamilton

President Washington's Cabinet

The president's **cabinet** is also part of the executive branch. The cabinet is not mentioned in the Constitution. It has formed over time. The cabinet is made up of the president's top advisors. Each one is appointed by the president and is responsible for a certain area of government. The following table displays a few examples.

Important Members of the President's Cabinet	
Secretary of State	The secretary of state is responsible for relationships with foreign countries.
Secretary of Defense	The secretary of defense is responsible for overseeing the US military.
Secretary of the Treasury	The secretary of the treasury is responsible for economic matters.
Attorney General	The attorney general is responsible for the nation's law enforcement.

THE JUDICIAL BRANCH: THE US SUPREME COURT AND FEDERAL COURTS

The **judicial branch** is made up of federal courts. These courts make sure that all laws follow the Constitution. If the judges on these courts believe that a law violates the Constitution, then they can strike down the law by declaring it "unconstitutional." The courts also make sure that the government does not violate the Constitution when enforcing the law.

The Supreme Court Building

John Jay   **John Marshall**

The judges on these courts are appointed by the president. The US **Supreme Court** is the highest court in the land. Nine judges sit on the Supreme Court. The lead judge is called the **chief justice**. The other eight judges are called **associate justices**. These justices have the authority to review the decisions of lower courts. The Supreme Court also has original jurisdiction (authority to hear a case first) over, "cases affecting ambassadors, other public ministers and consuls, and those in which a state shall be a party."

CHECKS AND BALANCES

The Constitution includes a system of **checks and balances**. Even though each branch has its own powers, they can still be "checked" by the other branches. For example, Congress has the power to make laws. The president, however, has to sign a bill before it becomes a law. Even if Congress passes a law and the president signs it, the judicial branch can still declare the law unconstitutional. The president can negotiate treaties and appoint officials (cabinet members, federal judges, and so on). However, the Senate must approve appointments and treaties before they become final. If a president, vice president, or other public official breaks the law, Congress has the power to impeach (charge with wrongdoing) that official and remove him or her from office. These are just a few examples of how checks and balances work. The purpose of checks and balances is to make sure that no branch of government becomes too powerful.

THE BILL OF RIGHTS

At first, a number of states would not accept the Constitution. Their leaders felt it did not do enough to protect civil rights. They feared that the national government would trample on peoples' freedoms. In order to convince these leaders to ratify the Constitution, the framers (leaders who drafted the Constitution) agreed to several **amendments** (changes to the Constitution). Following ratification, Congress presented twelve amendments to the states. The states ratified ten of them. These first ten amendments to the Constitution are known as the **Bill of Rights**.

FIRST AMENDMENT

The **First Amendment** guarantees several freedoms:

- **Freedom of speech** – People can say what they believe so long as it does not cause undue harm.

- **Freedom of the press** – The media has the right to report news freely and accurately.

- **Freedom to petition the government** – Citizens may insist that the government take certain actions.

- **Freedom to assemble** – Citizens may come together for rallies, protests, and other peaceful gatherings.

Freedom of the Press

- **Freedom of religion** – Citizens may practice any religion they want, so long as it does not interfere with others' rights. The government may not establish or support a state religion.

SECOND AMENDMENT

The **Second Amendment** protects citizens' right to bear arms (own guns).

THIRD AMENDMENT

Under the **Third Amendment**, US citizens cannot be forced to house US soldiers in times of peace, and only "in a manner prescribed by law" during times of war.

Colonial Militia

FOURTH AMENDMENT

The **Fourth Amendment** protects citizens from unlawful searches and seizures. No government agency can enter a citizen's home or search their property without proper authority.

FIFTH AMENDMENT

The **Fifth Amendment** states that no person may be, "deprived of life, liberty, or property without due process of law." Due process means that the government must follow the Constitution. It must respect an accused person's civil rights when arresting or putting that person on trial. It cannot punish someone for a crime or deny them any of their civil rights (taking away their freedom or property) without following the rules set by law. It also protects people from *double jeopardy* and *self-incrimination*. The government may not put a citizen on trial for the same

Due Process

crime more than once. Nor can it force accused people to testify against themselves in court. The Fifth Amendment also addresses *eminent domain*. The government may not take a citizen's property without paying them for it.

SIXTH AMENDMENT

The **Sixth Amendment** guarantees an accused citizen the right to a defense lawyer (a lawyer who defends accused people in court). It also promises them the right to a speedy jury trial. A jury is a group of citizens that hears all the evidence and decides a person's guilt or innocence. The Sixth Amendment also states that an accused person may confront

Jury Trial

witnesses. No one can testify against the accused secretly. The accused must be given a chance to question them. The accused may also call witnesses during a criminal trial.

SEVENTH AMENDMENT

Civil cases are different from criminal cases. In a criminal case, a citizen is accused by the government of committing a criminal act like murder, robbery, burglary, kidnapping, or so on. In a civil case, one private citizen or business accuses another private citizen or business of doing something wrong. Examples of a civil case include a patient suing a doctor for prescribing the wrong medicine, a landlord suing a renter for failing to pay rent, or a client suing a business for failing to stick to a signed contract. The **Seventh Amendment** states that civil defendants have the same right to a jury trial that criminal defendants have.

EIGHTH AMENDMENT

The **Eighth Amendment** protects citizens arrested or found guilty of a crime. It says that the government may not charge "excessive bail." Bail is money that accused people must pay to get out of jail until their trial. The Eighth Amendment also forbids "excessive fines." When someone is found guilty of a crime, a fine is money they have to pay as part of their punishment. Finally, the Eighth Amendment states that the government cannot use "cruel and unusual punishment."

Criminal Punishment in the Late 1700s

The government must punish guilty people in a way that fits with the crime. The US Supreme Court has ruled that it is okay to execute (put to death) people found guilty of first degree murder. However, it is not okay to execute someone found guilty of picking someone's pocket. The punishment would be far too severe for the crime.

NINTH AND TENTH AMENDMENTS

The **Ninth Amendment** states that the rights listed in the Bill of Rights are not the only ones citizens have. The **Tenth Amendment** says that all powers not given to the federal government or restricted by the Constitution belong to the states. It grants a certain amount of authority to state governments.

Practice 3.1: Framing the Constitution

1. The national body of laws that establishes the US government and guarantees citizens' rights is called the

   A. Articles of Confederation.

   B. US Constitution.

   C. Bill of Rights.

   D. Ten Amendments.

2. The branch of government responsible for making laws is called the

   A. legislative branch.

   B. executive branch.

   C. judicial branch.

   D. cabinet.

3. What are the first ten amendments to the Constitution called? Why did many people want these amendments added to the Constitution?

4. The fact that one branch makes the laws, another enforces the laws, and the third makes sure the laws are constitutional is an example of

   A. checks and balances.

   B. limited government.

   C. separation of powers.

   D. constitutional convention.

3.2 THE WAR OF 1812

CAUSES OF THE WAR

In 1812, the United States went to war with Great Britain again. There were several **causes of the war**. Many US citizens were upset that the British continued to impress US sailors. The British would capture US ships and force the sailors to serve in the British navy. In addition, Britain used its navy to interfere with US-French trade. (Great Britain was at war with France and did not want France to receive goods from the US). Native American resistance to US settlers moving

President James Madison

west also contributed to the war. Many along the western frontier felt that the British were encouraging and helping Native Americans to resist white settlers. Southerners also viewed Spanish Florida as a threat since Spain and Great Britain were allies.

NEW ENGLAND'S RESISTANCE

Not all US leaders favored war. New England's leaders opposed the war. New England depended on trade with Europe to carry on its business. Its leaders feared war would hurt New England's economy. The region almost seceded (left the Union) after the US declared war.

THE WAR

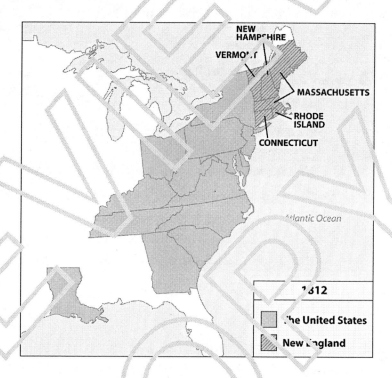

Andrew Jackson at The Battle of New Orleans

At times, it appeared that the US would lose the war. Early attempts to invade Canada failed. In August 1814, just months before the war ended, the British burned the White House, US Capitol, and much of Washington, DC. Fortunately for the Americans, the British were distracted for much of the war by their war with France in Europe. The US and Great Britain finally signed a treaty ending the war in late 1814. Andrew Jackson's victory at New Orleans in January 1815 helped end the fighting and made sure that the British stuck to the agreements in the treaty.

EFFECTS OF THE WAR

The War of 1812 increased **US nationalism**. Nationalism is pride in one's country. The war showed US citizens that they could stand up to a powerful country. The war was also good for **US business**. Once the war began, the US could not trade with European countries. As a result, US manufacturers learned to produce goods that the nation needed. US products improved and helped the US economy. The country stood more united after the war than it had before the war began.

Washington DC Burning

Practice 3.2: The War of 1812

1. Why did the US declare war on Great Britain in 1812?

2. What were some of the effects of the war?

CHAPTER 3 REVIEW

Key Terms, People, and Concepts

Articles of Confederation	judicial branch
United States Constitution	US Supreme Court
Constitutional Convention	chief justice
George Washington	associate justices
Benjamin Franklin	checks and balances
James Madison	amendments
compromise	Bill of Rights
Great Compromise	First Amendment
Three-fifths Compromise	Second Amendment
Slave Trade Compromise	Third Amendment
separation of powers	Fourth Amendment
legislative branch	Fifth Amendment
House of Representatives	Sixth Amendment
Senate	Seventh Amendment
Congress	Eighth Amendment
executive branch	Ninth Amendment
president of the United States	Tenth Amendment
vice president	War of 1812
Electoral College	causes of war
cabinet	effects of war

Multiple Choice Questions

Read the quote below, and answer the following question.

> "This body of laws is not enough. Our national government must have greater power. Why, under our current laws, we cannot even provide a national defense."
>
> US leader, 1786

1. The quote above is **most likely** talking about the

   A. United States Constitution.

   B. Declaration of Independence.

   C. Bill of Rights.

   D. Articles of Confederation.

2. Which of the following people is often called the "Father of the Constitution"?

   A. James Madison

   B. Thomas Jefferson

   C. George Washington

   D. Benjamin Franklin

3. The Great Compromise settled which of the following disputes?

   A. whether or not to continue the slave trade

   B. whether or not slaves should count as part of the population

   C. how the legislative branch should be structured

   D. how many justices should sit on the Supreme Court

4. The Three-fifths Compromise settled which of the following disputes?
   A. whether or not to continue the slave trade

   B. whether or not slaves should count as part of the population

   C. how the legislative branch should be structured

   D. how many justices should sit on the Supreme Court

5. Which of the following statements is **true**?
   A. The legislative branch may declare laws unconstitutional.

   B. Members of Congress are appointed by the president and must be approved by the Senate.

   C. The cabinet is elected at the same time as the vice president.

   D. The president is responsible for enforcing federal laws.

Look at the diagram below, and answer the following question.

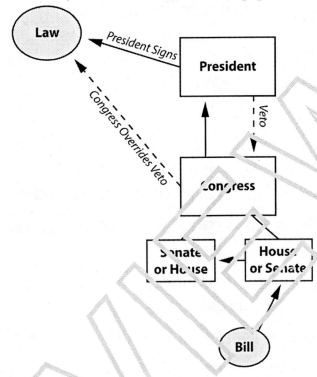

6. What process does the diagram above show?

A. an election

B. how federal laws are made

C. the Electoral College

D. how federal judges are appointed

7. The president has just appointed Margaret to be the new secretary of state. The Senate, however, refuses to approve Margaret's appointment. Therefore, Margaret will not get to be secretary of state. This is an example of

A. the electoral college.

B. a treaty.

C. checks and balances.

D. civil rights.

8. Citizens are guaranteed due process by the
   A. legislative branch.
   B. First Amendment.
   C. Articles of Confederation.
   D. Fifth Amendment.

9. Which of the following was a cause of the War of 1812?
   A. The American colonies wanted independence.
   B. US leaders felt the British were helping Native Americans fight US expansion.
   C. US leaders resented British soldiers attacking the United States' Native American allies.
   D. France would not let the US trade freely with Great Britain.

10. Which of the following was an effect of the War of 1812?
    A. Americans lost confidence and doubted that they could build a nation.
    B. Canada became part of the United States.
    C. The US lost Florida to Great Britain.
    D. Manufacturing improved.

Chapter 4
The United States: 1800 – 1861

This chapter addresses the following GPS-based CRCT standard(s):

SS4H6	The student will explain westward expansion of America between 1801 and 1861.
SS4H7	The student will examine the main ideas of the abolitionist and suffrage movement.

4.1 WESTERN EXPANSION

THE LOUISIANA PURCHASE

The Mississippi River divides the eastern and western United States. For centuries, the river has played an important role in travel and trade. It allows ships to sail back and forth between the Gulf of Mexico and inland North America. President Thomas Jefferson saw the importance of the Mississippi River. In 1803, he bought New Orleans and territory west of the Mississippi River from France. The deal became known as the **Louisiana Purchase**. It made New Orleans an important US city. It also opened the way to **western expansion**. Western expansion was the process of US settlers moving to areas west of the Mississippi.

LEWIS AND CLARK

In 1804, Meriwether Lewis and William Clark set out to find a water route to the Pacific Ocean. The **Lewis and Clark Expedition** played a major role in western settlement. The expedition followed the Missouri, Yellowstone, and Columbus Rivers. It also crossed the Rocky Mountains. Lewis and Clark's stories of adventure made others want to journey west. Many moved to the

Oregon Territory. (Today, the Oregon Territory is called the Northwest United States.) Many of these settlers followed a route known as the **Oregon Trail**.

TEXAS AND THE ALAMO

The Alamo

In 1821, Mexico gained control of **Texas**. In 1836, Texas declared **independence**. Mexican General Santa Anna responded with military force. On March 6, 1836, a small group of Texans stood against the Mexican leader at an old church called **the Alamo**. The Texans were very brave, but Santa Anna's forces were too strong. Every Texan who fought at the Alamo died in the battle or was executed after being captured.

The Texans later captured Santa Anna. The Mexican leader promised to give up Texas in exchange for his freedom. Once free, Texas asked to become part of the United States. President Andrew Jackson wanted to annex Texas, but he could not gain the support of northern states. Northerners knew that Texas would be a slave state. This would give slave states an advantage in Congress. Texas remained an independent nation until 1845.

CALIFORNIA AND GOLD

Miners

In 1848, settlers discovered **gold** in California. This caused the **California Gold Rush**. Large numbers of people rushed to California because they wanted to get rich. They became known as "49ers" because they arrived in 1849. Later, miners discovered gold in the Rocky Mountains as well. The Rockies produced even more gold than California, and mining soon became very important to the region. Small **mining towns** cropped up throughout the range. Many of them grew into bustling cities.

IMPACT OF WESTWARD EXPANSION ON NATIVE AMERICANS

Tribes Forced to Move

As settlers moved west, Native Americans suffered. The Plains Indians used buffalo for food, clothing, and shelter. Settlers and fur trappers killed many buffalo. By 1889, only a thousand buffalo were left. As a result, the Plains could no longer continue their way of life.

Many Native American tribes were forced to relocate to reservations. Reservations were pieces of land set aside for Native Americans. The US government forced Native Americans to move every time white settlers discovered gold or wanted more land. Large numbers of Native Americans died from being forced to travel great distances and move to reservations in lands they were not used to. Over time, Native Americans grew bitter and violent wars broke out. Famous battles occurred at Sand Creek, Little Bighorn, and Wounded Knee. In the end, the US government was too strong. By the end of the 1800s, the west was under US control.

IMPORTANT INVENTIONS

During the 1800s, **inventions** played an important role in western expansion.

Steamboats were boats powered by steam. Before steamboats, boats had to be powered by hand or wind. Steamboat travel was much faster. It increased trade and expansion by making it easier for goods and people to travel west. (See chapter 7, section 7.1)

The Steamboat

The **steam locomotive** was another important invention. Steam-powered trains led to the first cross-country railroads. Railroads allowed people to move west at a faster pace. They also allowed people and businesses to ship goods and resources. This opened new markets and helped the economy. (See chapter 7, section 7.1)

The **telegraph** helped people communicate. It let people send messages over long distances right away. People could live in the West and still communicate with the East. This contributed greatly to expansion. (See chapter 7, section 7.1)

Practice 4.1: Western Expansion

1. Which of the following statements describes the Louisiana Purchase?

    A. France bought Louisiana and other Midwestern territories from the United States.

    B. The United States bought New Orleans and territory west of the Mississippi River.

    C. The United States bought Louisiana and territory east of the Mississippi River.

    D. Lewis and Clark bought Louisiana from the United States in 1805.

2. As settlers moved west, Native Americans often
    A. married whites and lived with the settlers.

    B. lived peacefully among the whites.

    C. were forced to relocate to reservations

    D. became soldiers for the US government.

3. How did the steamboat impact expansion?
    A. decreased expansion by making it more difficult to travel by water

    B. increased expansion by making it easier for goods and people to travel

    C. did not impact expansion.

    D. led to the first long-distance travel by water.

4.2 ABOLITIONIST AND SUFFRAGE MOVEMENTS

ABOLITIONIST MOVEMENT

The **abolitionist movement** called for an end to slavery. In the 1830s, the abolitionist movement grew. Several key leaders arose out of this movement. They argued that slavery was cruel and should be stopped. Powerful southern landowners did not want slavery to end. They depended on slaves for labor. Many in the North, however, supported the abolitionist movement.

HARRIET TUBMAN

Harriet Tubman was an important African American abolitionist. She was an escaped slave who secretly returned to the South many times to help other slaves escape. The path she used was called the Underground Railroad. The **Underground Railroad** was a series of secret stops along a route that led north to free territory. Tubman helped many slaves make their way to freedom along the Underground Railroad.

The Underground Railroad

SUFFRAGE MOVEMENT

WOMEN'S SUFFRAGE AND ELIZABETH CADY STANTON

Elizabeth Cady Stanton

Many women wanted the same rights as men. This led to the **suffrage movement**. The suffrage movement demanded that women be given the right to vote. One of the movement's key leaders was **Elizabeth Cady Stanton**. Stanton helped organize the first women's rights convention in 1848. It was known as the Seneca Falls Conference. Between one hundred and three hundred people attended. Stanton used the conference to promote women's suffrage.

SOJOURNER TRUTH

Sojourner Truth was an African American abolitionist. She also supported women's rights. She was born a slave but escaped to freedom in 1826. She preached against slavery until her death in 1883. At the Ohio Women's Rights Convention in 1851, she gave a speech remembered as "Ain't I a Woman." In this speech, she pointed out the hardships she faced, both as a woman and an African American. Her passionate words had a powerful impact on the audience. Sojourner Truth contributed greatly to the abolitionist and women's rights movements.

Sojourner Truth

Practice 4.2: Abolitionist and Suffrage Movements

1. The abolitionist movement

   A. demanded that women be allowed to vote.

   B. was most often supported by southerners.

   C. called for an end to slavery.

   D. was the main topic at the Seneca Falls Conference

2. Who is **most** associated with the Underground Railroad?
   A. Sojourner Truth   C. Harriet Tubman

   B. Elizabeth Cady Stanton   D. William Clark

3. In 1851, who gave a famous speech remembered as "Ain't I a Woman?"
   A. Sojourner Truth   C. Harriet Tubman

   B. Elizabeth Cady Stanton   D. Eleanor Roosevelt

CHAPTER 4 REVIEW

Key Terms, People, and Concepts

Louisiana Purchase	impact of western expansion on Native Americans
western expansion	inventions
Lewis and Clark Expedition	steamboats
Oregon Territory	steam locomotive
Oregon Trail	telegraph
Texas	abolitionist movement
independence	Harriet Tubman
the Alamo	Underground Railroad
gold	suffrage movement
California Gold Rush	Elizabeth Cady Stanton
mining towns	Sojourner Truth

Multiple Choice Questions

1. What contributed **most** to the development of mining towns in the west?

   A. the discovery of gold

   B. the relocating of Native Americans

   C. the discovery of oil

   D. the invention of the steam locomotive

2. During the California Gold Rush,

   A. large numbers of Native Americans went to California in search of gold.

   B. thousands of people moved out of California.

   C. many people moved to California hoping to get rich.

   D. the US government would not allow mining of gold.

3. What happened at the Alamo?
   A. People discovered gold.

   B. A group of Texans fought against Santa Anna.

   C. Native Americans were killed by white settlers.

   D. The United States purchased Louisiana.

4. The Oregon Trail was

    A. the route many settlers followed as they moved west.

    B. the secret route used to help slaves escape to freedom.

    C. the first water route that led to the Pacific Ocean.

    D. used to move Native Americans to reservations.

5. The suffrage movement

    A. contributed to the development of the Underground Railroad.

    B. called for an end to slavery.

    C. was led by African American men.

    D. demanded that women be allowed to vote.

6. Elizabeth Cady Stanton is **most** associated with

    A. the Underground Railroad.   C. women's suffrage.

    B. the "Ain't I a Woman" speech.   D. the abolitionist movement.

7. Harriet Tubman is **most** remembered for

    A. helping slaves escape along the Underground Railroad.

    B. her speech at the Seneca Falls Conference in 1848.

    C. organizing the Ohio Women's Rights Convention in 1851.

    D. being the first woman to vote.

8. What do Elizabeth Cady Stanton and Sojourner Truth have in common?

    A. They helped slaves escape north to their freedom.

    B. They were born as African American slaves.

    C. They argued that women should have the same rights as men.

    D. They wanted slavery to be legal in certain states.

Chapter 5
Geographic Understandings

This chapter addresses the following GPS-based CRCT standard(s):

SS4G1	The student will be able to locate important physical and man-made features in the United States.
SS4G2	The student will describe how physical systems affect human systems.

5.1 IMPORTANT PHYSICAL GEOGRAPHIC AND MAN-MADE FEATURES OF THE UNITED STATES

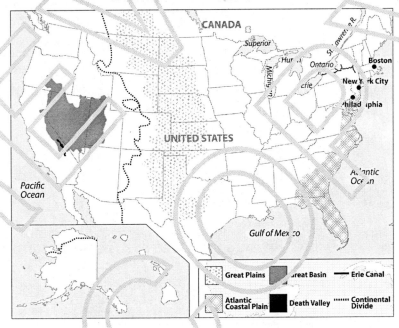

Geographic Features of the United States

The United States has many important physical geographic and man-made features. **Physical geographic features** are natural formations. Bodies of water, mountains, plains, forests, deserts, and gorges are all examples of natural features. **Man-made features** are features build by people. Cities, canals, monuments, and highways are examples of man-made features. Below are tables A and B. Table A lists some of the most important physical geographic features in the US. Table B lists some of the most important man-made features.

Table A IMPORTANT PHYSICAL FEATURES (see map on page 77)	
Atlantic Coastal Plain	The **Atlantic Coastal Plain** is the flatland area that runs along the coast of the Atlantic Ocean. It stretches from Florida north to New Jersey. During the colonial period, much of the Southern and Middle Colonies were located in the Atlantic Coastal Plain.
Great Plains	The **Great Plains** is the flatland prairie region that covers much of the Midwest United States. The region was home to Native American peoples like the Pawnee for many years before white settlers arrived. The Great Plains region covers parts of Montana, Wyoming, Colorado, Kansas, Nebraska, the Dakotas, Texas, New Mexico, and Oklahoma. **Native Americans in the 1800s**
Continental Divide	Rivers flow into oceans. In the United States, the **Continental Divide** marks the dividing line between bodies of water that flow into the Atlantic Ocean and those that flow into the Pacific. It runs along the Rocky Mountains from Canada to New Mexico. East of the Continental Divide, rivers flow towards the Atlantic. West of the Continental Divide, rivers flow towards the Pacific.
Great Basin	The **Great Basin** is a dry region covering parts of Utah, Nevada, and California. Because the basin does not have much water, Native Americans who lived in this region usually lived in smaller communities.
Death Valley	**Death Valley** is the lowest point in North America. It is extremely dry and very hot. The hottest temperature ever recorded in the Western Hemisphere was recorded in Death Valley. Death Valley is located in eastern California and parts of western Nevada. **Death Valley**

Great Lakes	The **Great Lakes** are five large lakes located in inland North America. Parts of southern Canada and the northern US make up their coastlines. The Great Lakes are Lake Michigan, Lake Superior, Lake Huron, Lake Ontario, and Lake Erie. They are some of the largest lakes in the world. Historically, the Great Lakes have been very important. They allow ships, traders, and settlers to reach parts of inland North America by water. Because of the access to shipping and trade the Great Lakes offer, many large cities have grown up along their shores. Chicago, Detroit, Cleveland, and Milwaukee are a few.  **Chicago on Lake Michigan**
St. Lawrence River	The **St. Lawrence River** has long been an important river. It connects the Great Lakes to the Atlantic Ocean. Without the St. Lawrence, inland trade would have been very difficult during the colonial period. Because it allowed explorers to travel back and forth between Europe and inland North America, control of the river became very important. The St. Lawrence became the site of the first permanent European colony in Canada—Quebec.

Map of the United States

Table B
IMPORTANT MAN-MADE FEATURES

New York City	**Manhattan Skyline**	New York City is the largest city in the United States. Historically, it has played a key role in commerce. It served as the nation's first capital and was the site of President Washington's first inauguration. Because of its location on the Atlantic coast, the city became a

popular arrival point for immigrants (people who move to the US from a foreign country). Immigration and industrialization (the growth of business and factories) caused New York's population to boom. Today, the city is home to many different types of people. New York serves as one of the world's major centers for business.

Boston	**Boston**, Massachusetts, became New England's biggest city and commercial center during the colonial period. It also became a place known for resisting British policies before the revolution. As a port city, Boston was home to a lot of trade and commerce. Since many British policies	**Colonial Boston**

affected colonial businessmen, many Bostonians became very angry at Britain for its tax and trade policies. Such anger led to events like the Boston Tea Party, which helped start the Revolutionary War.

| Philadelphia | Philadelphia, Pennsylvania, is another historic city. It is the largest city in Pennsylvania and, for a time, was the largest in the US. Like New York and Boston, its location helped make it an important city. Colonists |

| | relied on Philadelphia to provide a port for trade overseas. This brought lots of visitors to the city and allowed businesses of all types to thrive. Due to its central location in the colonies, Philadelphia became the center of government during the revolutionary period. Philadelphia is where the Declaration of Independence was signed in 1776. It is also where the Constitutional Convention drafted the US Constitution in 1787. After New York's brief time as the center of government, Philadelphia served as the nation's capital until the US built a new capital city—Washington, DC. |
| Erie Canal | A canal is a man-made waterway. The Erie Canal opened in 1825. It was important because it allowed boats to travel from New York City to the Great Lakes. This allowed businesses in New York to ship their goods west much more easily. Producers sold more and New York grew as an economic center. The canal also made it easier for people to travel, leading more settlers to move west. |

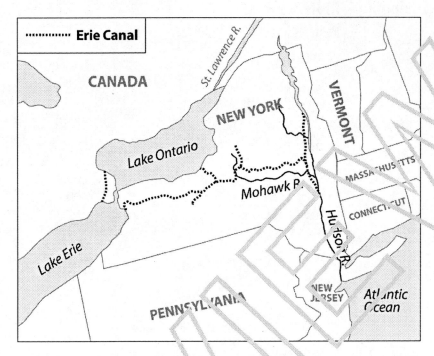

Route of the Erie Canal

Practice 5.1: Important Physical Geographic and Man-made Features of the United States

1. List the Great Lakes and tell why they have historically been important.

2. What city's geographic location helped make it the center of government before, during, and for several years after the American Revolution?

   A. New York

   B. Boston

   C. Philadelphia

   D. Washington, DC

3. What natural feature has played a major role in history by linking the Atlantic Ocean to the Great Lakes?

   A. Erie Canal

   B. St. Lawrence River

   C. Continental Divide

   D. Atlantic Coastal Plain

Look at the picture below and answer question #4.

4. This picture **most likely** shows Native Americans in

A. the Great Plains.

C. Death Valley.

B. the Great Basin.

D. the Atlantic Coastal Plain.

5.2 PHYSICAL GEOGRAPHY'S EFFECT ON HUMAN SYSTEMS

GEOGRAPHY'S EFFECT ON EARLY NATIVE AMERICANS

In chapter 1, we read how the environment affected Native Americans (review chapter 1, section 1.1). Physical geographic features are part of the natural environment. Native Americans who lived in forest regions, close to rivers, or along coasts, tended to build **permanent settlements** (they did not move

Early Native American Society

around) because many of the resources they needed were already available. Forests provided animals and vegetation for food. They also provided wood and stones for shelter and tools. Rivers, lakes, and oceans provided water for fishing and farming. Natural barriers were also important. Mountains and thick forests made it difficult for large groups to migrate (move). This also led to permanent settlements.

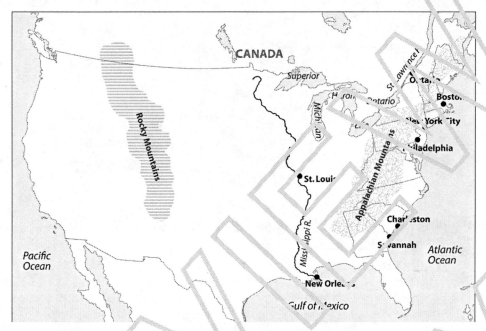

Native Americans of the Great Plains did not have as many resources as other Native American groups. They often lived **nomadic lifestyles** (they moved around). They depended on the buffalo and often followed herds wherever they went. The open plains also allowed the Native Americans of this region to travel freely, without having to worry about crossing thick forests or high mountains. As we learned in chapter 1, the environment, including physical features, impacted Native Americans' culture.

GEOGRAPHY'S EFFECT ON EARLY EUROPEAN EXPLORERS AND COLONIES

Early European explorers faced many challenges in North America. One was the physical environment. Most early North American colonists build settlements along inland waterways (rivers or lakes) or coastlines. These areas were easier to reach and allowed the colonies to trade with countries in Europe. It was many years before Europeans crossed natural barriers like the Appalachian Mountains, Mississippi River, or Rocky Mountains. These barriers made travel hard, and crossing them could be dangerous. Not until colonists began to understand that there were valuable resources, such as gold and abundant land, on the other side of these barriers, did settlers begin to move west in large numbers.

European explorers and settlers had to **adapt** (change the way they lived) in order to survive. They learned to build shelter out of available resources. They hunted animals that lived in the regions they settled. They learned how to farm crops that would grow in the climates where they lived. In colonies like Virginia and Massachusetts, many of the earliest settlers died because of their failure to adapt. They starved, died of diseases, or froze to death. Native Americans often helped early settlers by teaching them what crops to grow and how to deal with their natural environment. As time went on, colonists learned how to live better in their new surroundings, and fewer of them died or got sick.

GEOGRAPHY'S EFFECT ON ECONOMIC ACTIVITY

Physical geography also affected the **economic activity** in each colony (review chapter 1, section 1.2 and 1.3). French settlers took advantage of key rivers and inland waterways to trade fur. In the Southern Colonies, the climate and land made cash crops very important. The region came to rely heavily on plantations and slavery. Meanwhile, the many inland waterways

Southern Plantation

meant that landowners could ship goods without having to transport them to port cities. Few large cities grew up along the southern coast. The abundance of lumber and naval stores (tar, pitch, and other things important for making wooden ships) also made these resources important parts of the southern economy.

Northern Business

The Middle Colonies had more business and commerce. Lack of inland waterways led to a greater need for cities like Philadelphia and New York. These cities grew to be important economic centers. Farmers grew crops in the Middle Colonies, but they tended to need less labor. Slavery did not become as economically important in the Middle Colonies as it did in the South.

In New England, heavy reliance on Boston and the Atlantic coast made commerce, shipbuilding, and fishing very important to the region. The lack of cash crops also meant that farming was not the center of the economy the way it was in the South.

GEOGRAPHY AND SLAVERY

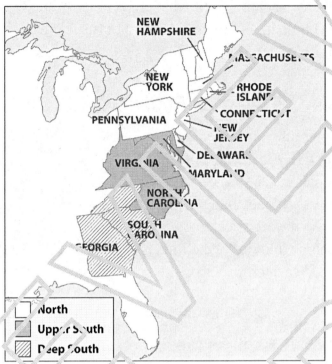

Since geography affected economic activity, it also affected slavery. The Lower South (South Carolina, parts of North Carolina, and Georgia) relied heavily on slavery because of their cash crops. Rice and indigo required a lot of labor. Later, as cotton became important and landowners established plantations further west, slavery became even more important to the Lower South's economy. In the Upper South (Virginia, Maryland, and parts of North Carolina), slavery was also important due to cash crops. However, over time, landowners in the Upper South worried that their slave population was getting too high. They feared a slave rebellion. Leaders in the Upper South successfully helped end the African slave trade. Once the African trade ended, the Upper South benefited economically from a domestic slave trade (business of shipping slaves from one part of the United States to another). Slave dealers in the Upper South sold slaves to traders who carried them west. These traders then sold the slaves to landowners in the Lower South who wanted them to work on plantations. Slavery remained important to the economies of the Lower South and Upper South until the end of the Civil War.

In the Middle Colonies and New England, slavery became less important. These regions did not rely as heavily on cash crops. The crops they did grow did not require as much labor. As cities grew, the northern economy relied more and more on business, trade, commerce, and industry. Over time, northern leaders began to oppose slavery. Disagreements over slavery led to the Civil War. This is just one example of how physical geography has affected US history.

GEOGRAPHY AND THE AMERICAN REVOLUTION

During the American Revolution, both the Continental Army and the British tried to use physical geography to help them win. In early 1776, General George Washington's troops seized high ground in Massachusetts. It is very difficult to win a battle against an enemy that is on high ground because an army has to attack uphill. Washington's position also

Battle of Bunker Hill

meant that the British were in danger because the Americans could easily fire cannons down at them, while remaining out of reach of cannons the British might try to fire up. Because Washington's army had the high ground, the British had to leave Boston and the Americans won an early victory.

Nathaniel Greene

Since the British army was larger, much better trained, and more powerful than the Continental Army, British commanders tried to force the Americans to fight on open fields. They believed they could beat the poorly trained Americans in a face-to-face battle. Early in the war, the Americans knew they could not win open-field battles. They hid behind trees and rocks. The Americans would strike quickly and then run away. By using geography to their advantage, the Americans frustrated the British. British forces sometimes used up their supplies chasing the American forces over many miles, trying to force them to fight on open ground.

Washington Crossing the Delaware

George Washington was a master at using geography to his advantage. When greatly in need of a victory in 1776, Washington crossed the Delaware River and surprised his enemy at Trenton, New Jersey. The attack was surprising because it happened in the dead of winter and the river was frozen. Washington knew no one would expect an army to cross a frozen river in the middle of the night. A few years later, in October 1781, Washington again used geography. He learned that British General Cornwallis was at Yorktown, Virginia. Yorktown sat on a peninsula (land area surrounded by water on three sides). Washington marched to Yorktown and trapped Cornwallis between the Continental Army and the Atlantic Ocean. The French navy made sure that no British ships came to Cornwallis' rescue.

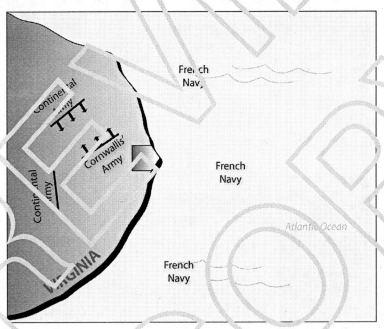

Finally, the location of the colonies themselves helped the Americans win the war. North America is very far away from Great Britain. It was very expensive and difficult for England to continue sending men and supplies to fight the war. Even though Great Britain's military was stronger, the British did not want to keep fighting for land so far away. They felt they had more important needs closer to home. Great Britain signed a treaty surrendering in 1783.

GEOGRAPHY'S EFFECT ON TERRITORIAL EXPANSION

GEOGRAPHIC OBSTACLES

Physical geography affected territorial expansion in North America. **Territorial expansion** was the process of white settlers occupying more and more land. **Geographic obstacles** are geographic features that make expansion difficult. Early on, most white settlers lived along the Atlantic coast, east of the Appalachian Mountains. The **Appalachian Mountains** run from North Georgia to Maine. They presented challenges

Daniel Boone Crossing the Appalachians

to early settlers because of their height and thick woodlands. Most dared not cross them. Eventually, people wanted the rich land beyond the Appalachians. With the help of explorers like Daniel Boone, settlers began crossing the Appalachians into lands further west.

Western Forest

The Great Plains

Thick forests and the Great Plains slowed westward expansion. Forests were difficult for large groups of people to travel through. They also required lots of labor to settle. Even those that did venture into forest regions had to make sure they settled close to bodies of water so that they could have water and access to travel and trade.

Before new farming technology arrived in the nineteenth century, the **Great Plains** of the Midwest were considered to be a vast desert. Farmers did not know how to farm them or how to adapt to the lack of wood and other resources for building homes.

For years, US settlers viewed the **Mississippi River** as a natural barrier to westward expansion. The Mississippi runs all the way from the Gulf of Mexico to Minnesota. Before 1803, the United States only stretched as far as the Mississippi River. After the Louisiana Purchase (review chapter 4, section 1.4), the river became the unofficial dividing line between the eastern and western United States. It is important to remember, however, that while the Mississippi River was seen as an obstacle to westward expansion, it actually helped north-south travel because it provided a natural trade route connecting the Atlantic Ocean to inland North America. For this reason, several of the United States' major cities are located along the Mississippi.

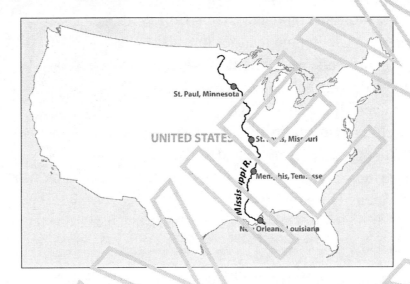

The **Rocky Mountains** were another obstacle. They run from New Mexico into Canada. The Spanish were the first Europeans to reach the Rockies. The Rockies high altitude and intensely cold winters made them very difficult, and sometimes deadly, to cross. Francisco de Coronado explored the region in the 1500s. It was over two hundred years later before European settlers started moving to the area to search for gold.

Rocky Mountains

GEOGRAPHIC GATEWAYS

Geographic gateways are geographic features that made territorial expansion easier.

The biggest gateways were rivers that allowed people to follow water routes west. The **Ohio River** helped settlers expand into the Northwest Territory (review chapter 4, section 4.1). The **Missouri River** helped adventurers like Lewis and Clark journey west. Meanwhile, natural passages through mountain areas helped expansion too. The **Cumberland Gap** was a passage that many settlers used to make their way through the Appalachian Mountains. (Review chapter 4, section 4.1 for more about westward expansion.)

Practice 5.2: Physical Geography's Effect on Human Systems

1. Due to the lack of resources like forests, Native Americans of the Great Plains often

   A. built settled communities.

   B. lived nomadic lifestyles.

   C. ate only vegetables.

   D. relied on fishing to survive.

2. Learning to grow crops, build houses using available resources, and live in unfamiliar climates are all ways early European explorers and settlers

   A. expanded west.

   B. crossed the Mississippi River.

   C. adapted to survive.

   D. changed their environment.

3. Which of the following is an example of how geography affected the economic activity of early colonies?

   A. The South grew cash crops.

   B. The North was colder.

   C. Native Americans relied on their environment to survive.

   D. Slaves existed in every colonial region.

4. During the early 1700s, the Appalachian Mountains, Great Plains, and Rocky Mountains were all

   A. gateways to westward expansion.

   B. regions heavily populated by British colonists.

   C. part of the United States.

   D. obstacles to expansion.

CHAPTER 5 REVIEW

Key Terms, People, and Concepts

physical geographic features

man-made features

Atlantic Coastal Plain

Great Plains

Continental Divide

Great Basin

Death Valley

Great Lakes

St. Lawrence River

New York City

Boston

Philadelphia

Erie Canal

geography's effect on Native Americans

permanent settlements

nomadic lifestyles

geography's effect on early European explorers

adapt

geography's effect on economic activity

geography's effect on the American Revolution

territorial expansion

geographic obstacles

Appalachian Mountains

thick forests

Great Plains

Mississippi River

Rocky Mountains

geographic gateways

Ohio River

Missouri River

Cumberland Gap

Multiple Choice Questions

Look at the map below and use it to answer questions 1 – 4.

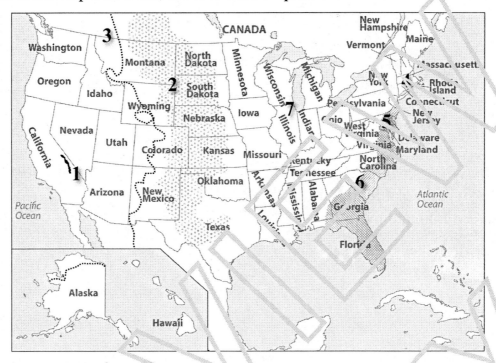

1. Where would one likely find the hottest and driest environment?

   A. 1   B. 2   C. 3   D. 4

2. In the 1700s and 1800s, where would one have found an economy based on cash crops?

   A. 2   B. 6   C. 7   D. 5

3. Which area served as the center of government during the American Revolution because of its central location in the colonies?

   A. 5   B. 7   C. 6   D. 3

4. Areas 5 and 6 are located in the
   A. Appalachian Mountains.   C. Atlantic Coastal Plain.

   B. Great Plains.   D. Great Basin.

5. Which of the following made early westward expansion easier?
   A. Appalachian Mountains   C. Continental Divide

   B. Cumberland Gap   D. forest regions

6. Which of the following made early westward expansion harder?
   A. Cumberland Gap   C. Lewis and Clark Expedition

   B. Missouri River   D. Rocky Mountains

7. What geographic feature did General George Washington use to help him win the Battle of Yorktown in 1781?
   A. high ground   C. Atlantic Ocean

   B. Delaware River   D. French navy

Chapter 6
Government and Civics

This chapter addresses the following GPS-based CRCT standard(s):

SS4CG1	The student will describe the meaning of: natural rights, "We the people," and the federal system of government in the US.
SS4CG2	The student will explain the importance of freedom of expreddion as written in the First Amendment to the US Constitution.
SS4CG3	The student will describe the function of government.
SS4CG4	The student will explain the importance of Americans sharing certain central democratic beliefs and principles, both personal and civic.
SS4CG5	The student will name positive character traits of key historic figures and government leaders (honesty, patriotism, courage. trustworthiness).

6.1 KEY PRINCIPLES OF US GOVERNMENT

NATURAL RIGHTS

The leaders who founded the United States are often called the **Founding Fathers**. The Founding Fathers believed that citizens are born with **natural rights**. Natural rights are rights that people have because they are human beings. It is wrong for governments to limit them. If a government violates natural rights, then the Founding

Constitutional Convention

Fathers believed the government should be replaced. The Declaration of Independence states that all people have a natural right to "life, liberty, and the pursuit of happiness."

THE FIRST AMENDMENT

One of the most important rights guaranteed by the US Constitution is **freedom of expression**. Under the **First Amendment**, citizens are free to express themselves in different ways. The First Amendment guarantees:

- **Freedom of Religion** – People are free to practice their own religion.

- **Freedom of Speech** – People may say what they want to, unless the government can prove their words would cause danger or harm.

- **Freedom of the Press** – Citizens and news agencies may print what they want unless the government can prove that what they write would violate someone else's rights.

- **Freedom to Assemble** – Citizens have the right to gather for peaceful purposes that do not violate the rights of others.

- **Freedom to Petition the Government** – Citizens have the right to complain to the government and call on their leaders to make changes.

Freedom of Religion

The Right to Assemble

"WE THE PEOPLE"

The **United States Constitution** is the country's national set of laws. It establishes the US government and states how the government works. It also protects the rights of citizens. The Founding Fathers based the Constitution on a belief in **limited government**. The government cannot do whatever it wants. It must obey the Constitution and respect the rights of citizens.

The Constitution begins with a sentence called the **Preamble**. The Preamble states the purpose of the document. The Preamble begins with the words: "We the people..." The writers of the Constitution wanted a government established by the people. They believed that leaders should rule by the **consent of the governed**. The people give the government its power. If the people are not pleased with their leaders, then they have the right to replace them. The people rule by **popular sovereignty** (the majority elects leaders to represent them and rule on their behalf).

We the People of the United States, in Order to form a more perfect Union, establish Justice, insure domestic Tranquility, provide for the common defence, promote the general Welfare, and secure the Blessings of Liberty to ourselves and our Posterity, do ordain and establish this Constitution for the United States of America.

The Preamble to the Constitution

FEDERALISM

The United States government depends on **federalism**. Federalism is a system that divides power between two levels of government: the national (federal) government and fifty state governments. Powers that belong only to the federal government are called **delegated powers**. Powers that belong only to state governments are **reserved powers**. Powers that are shared by both levels of government are called **concurrent powers**.

The US Capitol Building

Georgia's Capitol Building

Delegated Powers	Reserved Powers	Concurrent Powers
raise an army	manage public education	impose taxes
sign treaties	oversee elections	build roads
carry on foreign trade	regulate licenses	pass laws

Practice 6.1: Key Principles of US Government

1. Rights which people are born with and which the government has no right to take away are called

   A. natural rights.

   B. expression rights.

   C. protected rights.

   D. reserved rights.

2. Which of the following principles is expressed in the Preamble?

   A. freedom of speech

   B. freedom of expressin

   C. consent of the governed

   D. federalism.

3. Limited government means that

   A. some powers belong to the federal government and some belong to the states.

   B. the government must obey the Constitution and respect citizens' rights.

   C. the Constitution does not give the government much power.

   D. the national government has only reserved powers.

6.2 THE FUNCTIONS OF GOVERNMENT

MAKING AND ENFORCING LAWS

President Bush Signing a Law

The government makes and enforces laws. **Laws** are rules of society that every citizen is expected to obey. Citizens who break the law usually face some form of punishment. Laws **protect rights**. The government must make sure that no citizen's constitutional rights are violated. Laws must also **manage conflicts**. Sometimes, citizens, businesses, or groups don't get along. The government passes laws to make sure that such conflicts are settled peacefully.

In the United States, the federal and state governments are divided into three branches: legislative, executive, and judicial. The **legislative branch** is a body made up of elected officials. Its role is to make the laws. The **executive branch** is headed by an elected executive, such as the president or state governor. The executive branch is responsible for enforcing the laws

Congress in Session

(making sure people follow the laws). The **judicial branch** is made up of courts. The judges who are over these courts may be elected or appointed (given their post by an executive or higher judge). The judicial branch makes sure that laws passed by the legislative branch do not violate the rights of citizens.

At the federal level, the United States **Congress** serves as the legislative branch. Congress includes two houses. The **House of Representatives** is made up of representatives from each state. How many representatives a state has depends on population. The more people live in a state, the more representatives that state has. Representatives to the House serve two-year terms. The US **Senate** is made up of two senators from each state. Senators serve six-year terms. When a member of Congress introduces a **bill** (idea for a new law), members of the legislative branch vote on whether or not the bill should be a

HOW BILLS BECOME LAWS

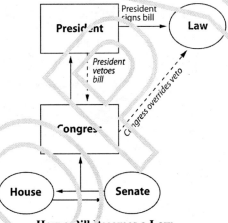
How a Bill Becomes a Law

law. If the majority votes for the bill, the bill goes to the other house. If the other house also votes for the bill, the bill goes to the president. If the president signs the bill, it becomes a law. If the president does not sign the bill, it is called a **veto**. A veto means that the bill does not become law *unless* two-thirds of the senators and two-thirds of the representatives in Congress vote in favor of the bill again. If two-thirds of both houses approve the bill after a veto, it is called an **override**. If Congress overrides the president's veto, the bill becomes a law anyway.

The **president of the United States** is the nation's chief executive. Once a law passes, it is the president's job to make sure it is enforced. The federal courts make up the judicial branch. The **US Supreme Court** is the highest court in the country. Federal judges are not elected. The president appoints them (gives them their job). Before they take office, however, the Senate must approve them (agree with the president's decision).

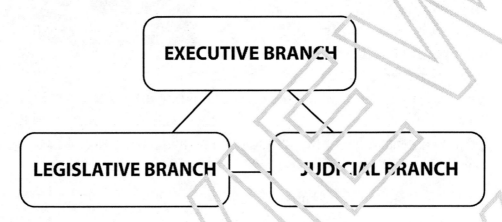

Three Branches of Government

MAINTAINING A NATIONAL DEFENSE

The United States government must maintain a **national defense**. The government must protect citizens against threats from outside the country. The US Army, Navy, Air Force, Marine Corps, and Coast Guard are all military forces that help protect the United States. The US government also pays private businesses to make weapons and supplies needed for national defense. Without a strong national defense, the United States would not be able to defend itself if it were attacked by another country.

| US Army Logo | US Air Force Logo | US Navy Logo |

FISCAL RESPONSIBILITY

The government needs money. It uses money to build roads, provide national defense, fund education, carry out government duties, and pay government workers. The number one way the government raises money is through taxes. **Taxes** are money that people and businesses must pay the government. The government has a **fiscal responsibility** to spend money wisely. Since political leaders tend to disagree over what is most important, they often argue over how to tax and spend money.

LIMITING THE POWER OF LEADERS

In chapter 3, we read about separation of powers and checks and balances (review chapter 3, section 3.3). The purpose of both is to prevent a leader or body of leaders from becoming too powerful. Another way of limiting the power of leaders is **term limits**. Term limits keep the same people from serving in the same office over and over again. In 1951, the states ratified the Twenty-second Amendment. It limits people who serve as president to only two terms in office. Many state governments have term limits for their governors. There are no term limits for representatives to the House or senators in the US Senate.

Practice 6.2: The Functions of Government

1. Explain how a bill becomes a law. What is a veto? How can a bill still become a law if there is a veto?

2. List three responsibilities of the national government.

6.3 TRAITS OF GOOD CITIZENSHIP

PROMOTING THE COMMON GOOD

There are several ways citizens promote the **common good** (what is best for society). Below is a list of several ways people practice positive citizenship.

Community Activism

- **Respect the Rights of Others**: Good citizens recognize and respect the rights of others. They do not try to limit the rights of others to free speech, freedom of religion, or any of the other rights guaranteed by the Constitution.

- **Obey Laws**: Good citizenship usually involves obeying laws. Laws are meant to protect people. They also help manage conflicts peacefully. If people do not follow the law, society has a hard time functioning. There have been times when the government passed unjust laws. There were once laws that allowed slavery or denied equal rights to minorities. In these and other cases, many good citizens protested and refused to obey the government until it changed the law.

- **Community Activism**: Doing things to make the community better is a great way to be a positive citizen. Volunteering to serve those in need or help with community projects are just a couple of ways citizens can be active in their own communities.

PARTICIPATING IN DEMOCRACY

The United States of America is a **democracy**. Citizens have a voice in their government. They elect the leaders who represent and serve them. Citizens take part in democracy in several ways.

- **Staying Informed**: Responsible citizens learn about issues that affect their lives. Being informed helps citizens make wise decisions about their government. Citizens use newspapers, magazines, television news broadcasts, radio, and the Internet to stay informed.

Citizen Reading a Newspaper   **Citizen Voting**

- **Voting**: Voting in elections is one of the ways people have a say in their government. They can vote for the candidate (person running for office) they think will do the best job. When citizens don't vote, they are giving up their right to have a voice in who leads their country, state, or community.

- **Volunteering**: Many citizens will volunteer to help with elections. Some work to help spread the word about candidates. Without volunteers, it would be difficult to conduct elections and many citizens would remain uninformed.

- **Communication**: US citizens have the right to communicate with public officials. Citizens may write, call, or email their representative in Congress or senator. They may also present petitions. A **petition** is a document asking the government to do something. Citizens often get hundreds, or even thousands, of people to sign petitions. The more people sign a petition, the more likely it is that the government will take action.

POSITIVE CHARACTER TRAITS

Character traits are things that make you the person you are. Your character determines how you act, treat other people, and handle things that happen. Great leaders and citizens have **positive character traits**. A few positive character traits are listed below.

George Washington

- **Honesty**: Honest people tell the truth. They make good friends and leaders because people know they can believe what honest people say.

- **Trustworthy**: Trustworthy people are honest and can be trusted to do what they say they will do. They can be trusted with money and responsibilities. Trustworthy leaders and citizens inspire others with confidence.

- **Patriotism**: Patriotism means to love one's country. Good leaders care more about their country and its citizens than they do themselves.

- **Courage**: People show courage when they are willing to do scary things for noble causes. Native Americans who fought stronger armies to protect their land, colonists willing to fight for independence during the revolutionary war, and freed slaves who exercised their civil rights despite threats and violence all showed great courage.

Harriet Tubman

Practice 6.3: Traits of Good Citizenship

1. What are three things citizens can do to promote the common good?

2. Reading the newspaper to learn about political issues, volunteering to help with an election, and starting a petition to get the local government to hire more police officers are all ways citizens

   A. prove they are honest.

   B. support their favorite candidates.

   C. take part in democracy.

   D. show courage.

3. Review the section above on positive character traits. Pick three of the people we read about in chapters 1-4 and describe how each showed one or more of these traits. See your teacher or test prep instructor for help if needed.

CHAPTER 6 REVIEW

Key Terms, People, and Concepts

Founding Fathers

natural rights

freedom of expression

First Amendment

freedom of religion

freedom of speech

freedom of the press

freedom to assemble

freedom to petition the government

United States Constitution

limited government

Preamble

consent of the governed

popular sovereignty

federalism

delegated powers

reserved powers

concurrent powers

laws

protect rights

manage conflicts

legislative branch

executive branch

judicial branch

Congress

House of Representatives

US Senate

bill

veto

override

president of the United States

US Supreme Court

national defense

taxes

fiscal responsibility

term limits

common good

respecting the rights of others

obeying laws

community activism

democracy

staying informed

voting

volunteering

communication

petition

positive character traits

Multiple Choice Questions

1. On Election Day, Benny takes part in the election and makes his choices for who he thinks should serve as leaders. Benny has

   A. served as a community activist.

   B. voted.

   C. volunteered.

   D. exercised his freedom of the press.

2. Which of the following is guaranteed under the First Amendment?
   A. Mary's right to own a gun.

   B. Jamaal's right to drive a car.

   C. McCall's right to disagree with Congress.

   D. Buddy's right to vote.

3. The idea that the US government's power is given by the people is expressed in
   A. the First Amendment.

   B. federalism.

   C. concurrent powers.

   D. the Preamble.

Look at the diagram below and answer questions #4 and #5.

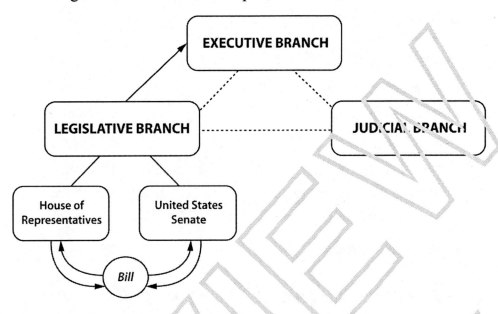

4. The diagram above shows what process?

   A. making federal laws.

   B. appointing judges to the Supreme Court.

   C. an election.

   D. freedom of expression.

5. If there is a veto in the process above, where should one draw an arrow in the diagram?

   A. from the executive branch to the judicial branch

   b. from the Senate to the House

   C. from the judicial branch to the executive branch

   D. from the executive branch to the legislative branch

6. Honesty, patriotism, trustworthiness, and courage are all

   A. forms of expression.

   B. positive character traits.

   C. guaranteed under the Constitution.

   D. delegated powers.

7. Both the state of Georgia and the United States government have the right to build highways in Georgia. This is an example of

   A. limited government.   C. delegated powers.

   B. reserved powers.   D. concurrent powers.

8. Barack Obama and John McCain are facing off in a national election to see who will be the president. Each state will come up with their own system for allowing citizens to vote. The state's authority over how elections are carried out is an example of

   A. reserved powers.   C. concurrent powers.

   B. delegated powers.   D. limited government.

9. The Constitution forbids leaders from passing laws against disagreeing with the president. This is an example of

   A. limited government.   C. federalism.

   B. consent of the governed.   D. popular sovereignty.

Chapter 7
Economic Understandings

This chapter addresses the following GPS-based CRCT standard(s):

SS4E1	The student will use the basic economic concepts of trade, opportunity cost, specialization, voluntary exchange, productivity, and price incentives to illustrate historic events.
SS4E2	The student will identify the elements of a personal budget and explain why personal spending and saving decisions are important.

7.1 BASIC ECONOMIC CONCEPTS IN US HISTORY

Economics is the study of how people, businesses, and countries spend their resources. **Resources** are things people use to buy or make things. Resources are limited. There are not enough resources for everything people want or need. Money is one limited resource. People use money to buy things. When people, businesses, or governments make **economic decisions**, they are deciding how to best spend limited amounts of money.

OPPORTUNITY COSTS

When a person, business, or government decides to spend money on one thing, they give up something else. The value of the thing they give up is called an **opportunity cost**. Say that Bill is hungry and thirsty. He has enough money to buy a hot dog or a soft drink. He does not have enough money for both. If Bill buys

Spending Money

the drink, then his opportunity cost is eating the hot dog. Eating the hot dog is what he gives up. If Bill buys the hot dog, then his opportunity cost is drinking the soft drink.

OPPORTUNITY COSTS IN HISTORY

Colonial Exploration

History is full of economic decisions and opportunity costs. Every time leaders or individuals made decisions, they had to give something up. When European nations decided to send **explorers to the New World** they were making economic decisions. They used money and resources for exploration that could have been spent on other things. Rulers decided that the wealth they could get from the Americas made exploration worth the opportunity costs.

MARKETS AND PRICE

Market Activity

A **market** is where economic decisions are made. **Goods** are products you can touch, like a shirt or a hamburger. **Services** are actions, like a medical check up or mowing the grass. Goods and services are bought and sold in markets. People buy groceries, cars, computers, clothes, houses, medical care, and many other things in a market. **Price** is the amount of money that **producers** (those who make and sell goods and services) sell goods or services for. Producers will only sell goods and services at a price that makes them money. In order to make money, producers must be able to sell their goods and services for more money than it cost them to make the good or service. The money that producers make after selling their good or service is called **profit**. Producers want to make as much profit as possible. However, they have to be careful not to charge too high a price. If the price is too high, **consumers** (those who buy goods and services) will not buy what they are selling.

Price incentives encourage people to buy or produce goods and services. Low prices are a price incentive to buy. Consumers are more likely to buy goods and services that are priced low. They can get more with less money. High prices are a price incentive to produce and sell. Producers will produce things they can sell at a high price. High prices produce more profits.

PRICE AND MARKET CONDITIONS IN US HISTORY

Colonial Merchant

Prices and markets have affected US history. European colonists came to the Americas for many different reasons (review chapter 1, section 1.2), but they all needed money to survive. Colonists had to make wise economic decisions. Those who lived in places where farming was most profitable tended to raise cash crops. Since cities had larger populations, people often opened shops or businesses to supply goods and services. Artisans with special skills made and sold the goods they crafted. People who lived along the coast relied on shipping and fishing. People decided how to earn a living based on resources and what price they could charge for their goods and services. Goods or services that yielded large profits (such as tobacco) attracted producers. Goods or services that yielded small profits were not as popular.

SPECIALIZATION

When a region, business, or person focuses on producing one thing, it is called **specialization**. Specialization helps economies. It leads to more production and better quality goods and services. During the colonial period, the Southern Colonies specialized in cash crops. Farmers in the Middle Colonies specialized in wheat and rye. In cities, artisans and merchants specialized in crafts and business. In New England, fishing and shipping were important. Rather than trying to produce

Cash Crops

everything, people and regions specialized in what they did best. They profited from the things they could most easily produce. This improved the standard of living in each colony.

ADVANTAGES OF TRADE AND VOLUNTARY EXCHANGE

Voluntary exchange is an important part of economics. Two things are necessary for voluntary exchange. First, producers must be free to choose what to make and sell. Second, consumers must be free to choose what to buy. Voluntary exchange helps both buyers and sellers. Since consumers are free to buy what they want, producers learn what goods and services are in demand. This helps sellers because they know what they should produce if they want to make a profit. Voluntary exchange also helps consumers by making sure producers only make things consumers want or need. It also keeps prices low because consumers can freely choose who to buy from.

NATIVE AMERICAN AND COLONIAL TRADE

Voluntary exchange helped pre-historic and colonial societies. Long before Europeans arrived, Native American populations often traded with one another. **Trade** happens when people from different villages, regions, or countries exchange goods. Trade allows people to get the things they want or need without having to make everything themselves.

Native American Trade

Colonial Trade with England

Trade helped the colonies and England during the colonial period. The colonies provided England with natural resources like rice, tobacco, and lumber. England could buy these goods more cheaply from the colonies than it could from other countries. English manufacturers (people who use resources to make things) used these goods to make products. England sold many of these products to colonists in America. This allowed Americans to buy goods that could not easily be made in the colonies.

ECONOMIC IMPACT OF TECHNOLOGY

New technology helps economic development. **Technology** is any machine or invention that makes production easier. Eli Whitney invented the **cotton gin** in 1793. It made cotton processing much faster and cheaper. The cotton gin helped make cotton the South's most important crop. Plantation owners got very wealthy, and the region grew to depend on slavery.

Steamboat

The **steamboat** was another key invention. Steam power allowed boats to travel faster. Steamboats did not rely on wind the way sail-powered ships did. By making water travel faster and easier, the steamboat helped businesses ship their products to more places. Producers made more money as new markets opened and businesses grew. People also moved west at a faster pace thanks to water routes like the Erie Canal (review chapter 5, section 5.1 for more information on the Erie Canal).

The **steam locomotive** (steam-powered train) also changed the US economy. Railroads allowed people to move goods and resources faster and more easily. Production increased. The growing western population created new places to buy and sell goods. The US economy grew. A few big business leaders got very rich. Many citizens' standard of living improved.

Steam Locomotive

The **telegraph** made communication easier. Before telephones or computers, the telegraph provided a way for people who were far apart to send messages to each other. Manufacturers could quickly learn what products were in demand in other parts of the country. People could carry on business with more people and in more places.

Practice 7.1: Basic Economic Concepts in US History

1. When Great Britain decided to pay for voyages to the New World, they spent money on ships and supplies that could have been spent to fight wars in Europe. Which of the following is the opportunity cost of such a decision?

   A. Great Britain's military

   B. land that could have been conquered had the British spent more money on European wars

   C. the land British explorers claimed in the New World

   D. the money spent on voyages that could have been used to fund wars in Europe

2. Which of the following is an example of a price incentive?

   A. Southern farmers grow more cotton because they can sell it for large profit.

   B. Northern citizens buy southern cotton because the price is high.

   C. Consumers refuse to buy a certain good until the price falls.

   D. A store tries to get people to buy more goods by staying open longer.

3. How does voluntary exchange help buyers and sellers?

4. Give three examples of technology, and tell how each invention affected the US economy.

7.2 PERSONAL FINANCES

MAKING A BUDGET

Making a Household Budget

Citizen needs to learn how to manage their own money. Having a budget is an important part of any money-management plan. A **budget** is a record of how you plan to spend your money. It helps keep you from spending too much. People who spend too much money end up falling into debt. **Debt** is the amount of money that you owe. People get in debt when they spend more money than they have and are forced to borrow to pay for things.

INCOME AND EXPENSES

The first step to making a budget is to know your **income**. Income is how much money you make. For most people, income is the amount of money they make at work. A regular allowance from your parents is also a form of income. It is important to know your income first so that you know how much money you are able to spend.

Once you know your income, the second step is to write down all of your **expenses**. Expenses are the things you spend money on. When you know your income and expenses, you can then decide how much income to spend on each expense. The key is to make sure that expenses are less than income. Once you have a budget that works, you then need to stick to it. Spend only what your budget allows because you know you can afford it. When people don't stick to a budget, they run the risk of getting into financial trouble.

SAVING MONEY

Saving Money

Spending means giving money in return for goods or services. You spend money to buy a video game, go to Six Flags, or buy a soda at the convenience store. **Saving** is taking money you *could spend* and putting it aside for a later time. People save money in different ways. Many put money in savings accounts. Savings accounts allow a person's money to gain interest. **Interest** is money that a borrower pays a lender for the use of money. When you put your money in a savings account, you are lending it to the bank. The bank uses it and pays you interest. Later, you can withdraw the money and interest (take it out of the bank).

Investing is one of the most popular ways people save money. When you invest, you allow businesses to use part of your money in return for interest or a share of their profits. It could be your own business that you invest in. Often, however, it is other peoples' businesses. People invest in different ways. Many buy stocks, which make them part owners of a company. Others buy bonds, which does not give

Buying a Home

them ownership but rather allows them to lend money to a business or institution. Many participate in mutual funds, which are made up of many companies. Mutual funds are safer because, if one company in the fund does poorly, others are usually doing well. Still others might invest in CDs (certificates of deposit) which keep their money in a special account for a set period of time. When the time expires, they withdraw the money with interest.

REASONS TO SAVE

There are lots of **reasons why people save**. Sometimes, they save because they want to buy something they can't afford to buy right away. Young couples often save to buy their first home. Teenagers often save to buy a car. Parents usually save to pay for their kids' college educations. Families might save to take a nice vacation. One of the most important things citizens save for is retirement. When a person retires, they no longer work. People may retire because they are sick or because they simply don't want to work anymore. The most common

Retirees

reason people retire is age. However, even retired people still need money to live on. If they are not working and earning a salary (money paid by an employer) then this money must come from somewhere else. For many it comes from retirement savings. Many people participate in retirement savings plans at work. Others set up IRAs (individual retirement accounts). IRAs allow people to save money over time for when they are older. The earlier people start such accounts, the longer their money grows. The longer their money grows, the more they have for retirement. Many people count on Social Security to provide their retirement income. Social Security is a federal government program that gives money to retired citizens. But Social Security does not provide enough money for most people to live on. Therefore, citizens need to save on their own as well. By investing wisely and starting early, people can do a good job of saving for retirement.

WHY SAVING IS IMPORTANT

Saving money is important for many reasons. People don't know what will happen in the future. They could lose their job, get hurt and be unable to work, have a huge expense that they did not plan on, or face other challenges. People who save money have an easier time dealing with such problems. Those that don't save often find themselves in trouble because they lack the money to deal with such challenges. Saving money takes discipline. It is usually more fun to spend. But wise and responsible citizens will save some of their income rather than spend all of it.

Practice 7.2: Personal Finances

1. Dudley makes $2500 a month working at Danbar, Inc. He pays $900 a month in rent and usually spends at least $1200 a month on other things. The remaining $400 a month goes in the bank. Which of the following statements is true?

   A. Dudley saves most of his income.

   B. Dudley's expenses equal $2500 a month.

   C. Dudley spends more than he makes.

   D. Dudley's expenses equal roughly $2100 a month.

2. If Amy wants to make sure that she spends less money than she makes, then she should

   A. make a budget.

   B. go into debt.

   C. forget about saving.

   D. borrow money.

3. Why is it important to save money?

CHAPTER 7 REVIEW

Key Terms, People, and Concepts

resources	technology
economic decisions	cotton gin
opportunity cost	steamboat
opportunity costs involved in exploration of the New World	steam locomotive
market	telegraph
goods	budget
services	debt
price	income
producers	expenses
profit	spending
consumers	saving
price incentive	interest
specialization	investing
voluntary exchange	reasons people save
trade	why saving is important

Multiple Choice Questions

1. When a nation decides how to spend its money, this is an example of

    A. an economic decision.

    B. exploration.

    C. opportunity costs.

    D. trade.

2. Michael's company makes the decision to produce tennis shoes instead of hockey sticks. The money Michael's company could have made producing hockey sticks is

    A. an opportunity cost.

    B. voluntary exchange.

    C. a price incentive.

    D. an example of specialization.

3. When the Native Americans chose to trade with one another, it was an example of

   A. price incentives.

   B. specialization.

   C. budget.

   D. voluntary exchange.

4. What effect does voluntary exchange usually have on buyers and sellers?

   A. It helps buyers but is bad for sellers.

   B. It helps sellers but is bad for buyers.

   C. It helps both buyers and sellers.

   D. It has little affect on buyers or sellers.

5. How does trade usually promote economic activity?

   A. It ends voluntary exchange.

   B. It gets rid of opportunity costs.

   C. It improves quality and production.

   D. It replaces specialization with voluntary exchange.

6. The steam locomotive's ability to make transportation easier and faster is one example of

   A. voluntary exchange.

   B. economic decision-making.

   C. technology's economic impact.

   D. how trade has benefited from specialization.

7. Brenda wants to buy a new shirt. However, she looks at her personal money plan and sees that she has already spent all her money for the month. She decides to wait until next month to buy the shirt. Brenda is

   A. avoiding opportunity costs.

   B. sticking to her budget.

   C. putting her money in savings.

   D. using technology.

Georgia 4 Social Studies
Practice Test 1

The purpose of this practice test is to measure your progress in Social Studies. This test is based on the GPS-based Georgia CRCT in Social Studies and adheres to the sample question format provided by the Georgia Department of Education.

General Directions:

1. Read all directions carefully.

2. Read each question or sample. Then choose the best answer.

3. Choose only one answer for each question. If you change an answer, be sure to erase your original answer completely.

Use the map below to answer questions 1 to 3.

1. Who explored the area marked 'W'?   SS4H2
    A. Juan Ponce de Leon   C. Samuel de Champlain

    B. Hernando de Soto   D. Henry Hudson

2. In which region on the map did Juan Ponce de Leon explore?   SS4H2
    A. W

    B. X

    C. Y

    D. Juan Ponce de Leon was not an explorer.

3. Who is **most** remembered for exploring the area marked Y?   SS4H2
    A. Hernando de Soto   C. Henry Hudson

    B. Christopher Columbus   D. Samuel de Champlain

4. The Great Basin is a   SS4G1

  A. dry region covering parts of Utah, Nevada, and California.

  B. flat area that covers a lot of the Midwest.

  C. flatland area that runs along the coast of the Atlantic Ocean.

  D. region in the South that is known for being very hot.

5. Who is **most** associated with the speech "Ain't I a Woman?"   SS4H7

  A. Elizabeth Cady Stanton

  B. William Clark

  C. Harriet Tubman

  D. Sojourner Truth.

6. In early 1776, what geographical feature did General George Washington use that forced the British to flee Boston?   SS4G2

  A. open fields

  B. a peninsula

  C. high ground

  D. the Delaware River

7. Limited government means that   SS4CG1

  A. the president does not have final authority in government issues.

  B. power is divided between the states and the federal government.

  C. the government must obey the Constitution and respect citizens' rights.

  D. the Bill of Rights gives most of the power to citizens.

8. Voluntary exchange tends to help   SS4E1

  A. sellers.

  B. buyers.

  C. neither sellers nor buyers.

  D. both sellers and buyers.

9. People who could not afford to come to North America on their own often became   SS4H3

  A. Quakers.

  B. convicts.

  C. indentured servants.

  D. Puritans.

10. What is the best heading for the list below? SS4H1
    - Inuit
    - Nez Perez
    - Hopi
    - Pawnee

    A. Native American Peoples of North America

    B. Leaders of Native American Tribes

    C. Religious Places of Worship for Native Americans

    D. Famous Spanish Explorers

11. On Election Day, Jack makes his choices for who he thinks should serve as the country's leaders. Jack has SS4C?4

    A. run for office.

    B. voted.

    C. volunteered.

    D. obeyed the law.

12. Who of the following was **not** a president of the United States? SS4H4

    A. George Washington

    B. Thomas Jefferson

    C. John Adams

    D. Benjamin Franklin

13. Which of the following is **not** a right guaranteed under the first amendment? SS4CG2

    A. Jamie can practice his own religion.

    B. Jennifer can say anything she wants to as long as it does not harm anyone.

    C. Melissa must be allowed to attend any school she wants.

    D. Mark can complain about the president.

14. Michael's ancestors were Native Americans. They lived in the Great Plains. Michael is **most likely** from which of the following people groups? SS4H1

    A. Pawnee.

    B. Seminole.

    C. Inuit.

    D. Hopi.

15. Which amendment to the Constitution protects citizens' freedom of speech? SS4H5

    A. First Amendment

    B. Second Amendment

    C. Third Amendment

    D. Fourth Amendment

Read the list below and answer the following question.

- Manage conflicts
- Protect people's rights
- Makes sure the Constitution is obeyed

16. What is the **best** heading for the list above? SS4CG3

    A. Duties of the Judicial Branch of Government
    B. The Fiscal Responsibilities of the Government.
    C. Decisions Made by the Federal Government
    D. Reasons the Government Makes Laws.

17. Brian works for a publishing company. Brian receives what for his labor? SS4E2

    A. bartering
    B. income
    C. inflation
    D. free trade

18. What led to the battle at the Alamo? SS4H6

    A. Texas declared itself independent from Mexico.
    B. Lewis and Clark refused to surrender Oregon.
    C. conflicts between Native Americans and settlers.
    D. General Santa Anna tried to take gold from settlers.

19. California's state government is responsible for the public education system. This is an example of SS4CG1

    A. reserved powers
    B. delegated powers.
    C. limited government.
    D. concurrent powers.

20. New York is SS4G1

    A. located on the Atlantic coast.
    B. the lowest point in America.
    C. where the Declaration of Independence was signed.
    D. the capital of the United States.

Use the map below to answer question number 21.

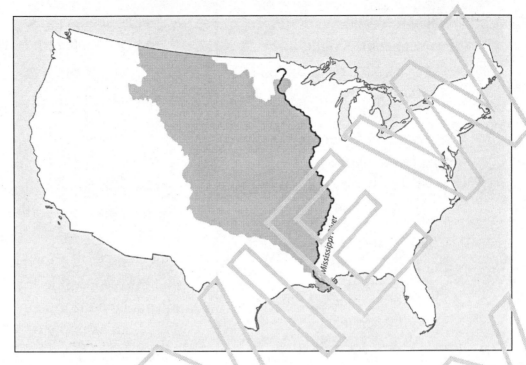

21. Which of the following is related to the area highlighted on the map above?

    A. the Compromise of 1850

    B. the Louisiana Purchase

    C. the Gold Rush of 1849

    D. the Alamo

22. Which branch of government is responsible for making laws?

    A. legislative

    B. executive

    C. judicial

    D. the president

23. The Kwakiutl settled in

    A. Georgia and Tennessee.

    B. southwest Canada and northwestern United States.

    C. the southeastern United States.

    D. large towns along the ocean.

24. Who is the list below describing?   SS4H2

- A Spanish explorer
- Discovered the "New World" in 1492
- Established Hispaniola

A. Juan Ponce de Leon

B. Samuel de Champlain

C. Jacques Cartier

D. Christopher Columbus

25. How did geography affect the economic activity of early colonies?   SS4G2

A. The North was much hotter.

B. The South grew cash crops.

C. The North relied on slavery.

D. Native Americans depended on their environment to survive.

26. Early Native Americans relied on their environment for   SS4H1

A. shelter.

B. clothing.

C. food.

D. all of the above.

27. The Cumberland Gap, the Ohio River, and the Missouri River   SS4G2

A. made territorial expansion easier.

B. made territorial expansion harder.

C. are all located in the Appalachian mountains.

D. were heavily populated by early British colonists.

28. The idea that the US government's power is given by the people is expressed in   SS4CG1

A. the First Amendment

B. the Preamble of the US Constitution.

C. federalism.

D. concurrent powers.

29. A price incentive   SS4E1

A. makes people not want to buy goods or services.

B. encourages people to buy or produce goods and services.

C. is made by consumers.

D. is used by the government to raise taxes.

Use the quotation below to answer the following question.

> Gentlemen, I believe that this compromise presents the best possible solution to this problem. Those in the North feel strongly that slaves are not citizens and therefore should not be counted in the population. Our southern representatives feel just as strongly that they should be, and I see no other solution.

30. What is the above quote most likely describing?   SS4H5

    A. the Slave Trade Compromise

    B. the Three-Fifths compromise

    C. the Great Compromise

    D. causes of the War of 1812

31. What happens to a bill if the president does not sign it?   SS4CG3

    A. It does not become a law unless two-thirds of each house vote in favor of the bill again.

    B. It never becomes a law.

    C. It only becomes a law if a majority of each house votes in favor of the bill again.

    D. It becomes a law anyway since the majority of Congress voted for it.

32. Jack was a Puritan living in Massachusetts. He lived in a   SS4H3

    A. Southern Colony.

    B. Middle Colony.

    C. New England Colony.

    D. Royal Colony.

33. Honesty, trustworthiness, and courage are all   SS4CG5

    A. guaranteed under the First Amendment

    B. forms of expression.

    C. positive character traits.

    D. reserved powers.

34. During the Boston Tea Party,   SS4H4

    A. colonists raided British ships and threw crates overboard.

    B. Native Americans threw tea at British troops.

    C. Americans celebrated their victory at Trenton.

    D. the cost of tea was very expensive.

35. Having a budget, investing for the future, and saving money are all ways citizens   SS4E2

   A. influence government spending.

   B. go into debt.

   C. manage their money wisely.

   D. spend more money than they make.

36. What do the Kwakiutl and Nez Perez have in common?   SS4H1

   A. They were originally from eastern regions of Canada.

   B. They lived in what is today the northwest United States.

   C. They settled in what is now the US southwest.

   D. They lived in the arctic regions of the north.

37. Which amendment protects citizens' right to bear arms?   SS4H5

   A. First Amendment

   B. Second Amendment

   C. Third Amendment

   D. Seventh Amendment

38. The Declaration of Independence states that all people have a natural right to   SS4CG1

   A. free speech.

   B. a trial by jury.

   C. the pursuit of happiness.

   D. worship as they choose.

Read the statement below and answer the following question.

> Women feel humiliation the same way the black man does. Even though we are not socially segregated, we are politically as isolated as the black man.

39. The above statement was made by Elizabeth Cady Stanton. Which of the following best describes its meaning?   SS4H

   A. Women suffer from inequality.

   B. Women have it worse than African Americans.

   C. White women should be segregated from black men.

   D. Minorities should be allowed to run for office.

Use the image below to answer the following question.

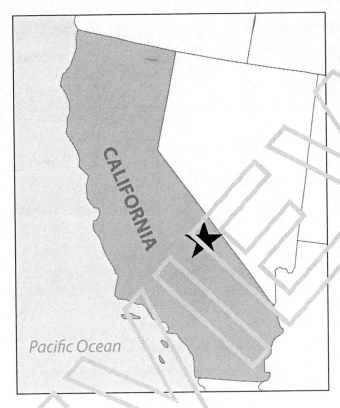

40. What does the star represent on the map?   SS4G1

   A. Erie Canal   C. Death Valley

   B. Lake Ontario   D. the St. Lawrence River

41. Robert reads the newspa-   SS4CG4
per every morning so he
can learn about important issues.
This helps him make wise decisions. This is called

A. obeying the law.

B. volunteering.

C. staying informed.

D. setting term limits.

42. Bobbi is suspected of   SS4H5
stealing clothes from a
department store. She has a right
to a defense lawyer and a trial by
jury. This is guaranteed by the

A. Second Amendment.

B. Third Amendment.

C. Sixth Amendment

D. Ninth Amendment.

43. The Federal government has a fiscal responsibility to   SS4CG3

    A. spend money wisely.

    B. control the economy.

    C. pass laws.

    D. build friendships with other countries.

44. Which of the following is an example of a price incentive?   SS4E1

    A. Producers refuse to make more goods until the cost of supplies drops.

    B. A Southern plantation owner grows more tobacco because he can sell it for a large profit.

    C. Northern citizens refuse to buy tobacco because the price is high.

    D. A company tries to improve production by changing location.

45. The Middle Colonies featured   SS4G2

    A. more slavery than the other colonies.

    B. more business and commerce than the southern colonies.

    C. mostly cash crops.

    D. a strong Puritan faith.

46. What do Ponce de Leon and Vasco Nunez Balboa have in common?   SS4H1

    A. They were French explorers.

    B. They were Native American leaders.

    C. They were Spanish explorers.

    D. They were the first Europeans to explore Georgia.

47. The escaped slave who secretly helped many other slaves make their way to freedom was   SS4H7

    A. Elizabeth Cady Stanton.

    B. William Clark.

    C. Harriet Tubman.

    D. Sojourner Truth.

48. Which of the following ideas is expressed in the Preamble?   SS4CG1

    A. federalism

    B. freedom of speech

    C. freedom of religion

    D. consent of the governed

49. Which region had more types of people and greater religious freedom than other colonies? `SS4H3`

 A. Massachusetts

 B. New England

 C. the Middle Colonies

 D. Royal Colonies

50. The route that many settlers followed west was called `SS4H6`

 A. the California Path.

 B. the Oregon Trail.

 C. Little Bighorn.

 D. the Underground Rairoad.

51. Citizens often help with elections. They spread the word about candidates or assist in election procedures. This is called `SS4CG4`

 A. volunteering.

 B. freedom to assemble.

 C. popular sovereignty.

 D. voting.

52. What is the best heading for the list below? `SS4H2`

 • Came to spread religion
 • In search of wealth
 • Wanted to be famous

 A. Reasons Why early African Americans came to America

 B. Reasons that Native Americans Moved to Europe

 C. Reasons European Explorers Came to America

 D. Reasons Ben Franklin returned to America after the Revolution

53. Who wrote most of the Declaration of Independence? `SS4H4`

 A. Patrick Henry

 B. Benjamin Franklin

 C. Thomas Jefferson

 D. John Adams

54. Which amendment guarantees due process? `SS4H5`

 A. First Amendment

 B. Fourth Amendment

 C. Tenth Amendment

 D. Fifth Amendment

Use the map below to answer questions 55 and 56.

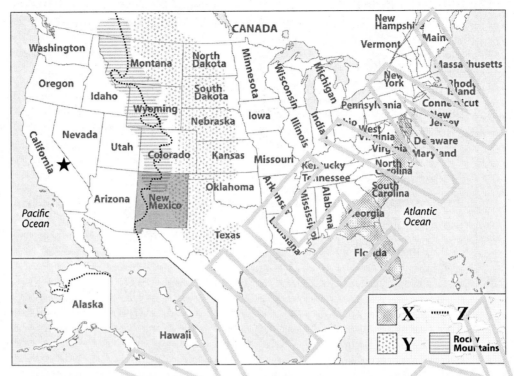

55. What does the letter X represent on the map?

    A. Death Valley   C. St. Lawrence River

    B. Atlantic Coastal Plain   D. Great Basin

SS4G

56. Which letter represents the Continental Divide?

    A. X

    B. Y

    C. Z

    D. The Continental Divide is not shown on the map

SS4G1

57. Early colonists who lived along the coast relied on

    A. hunting animals.

    B. cash crops.

    C. fishing and shipping.

    D. the fur trade.

SS4H

58. The arctic region is where the

    A. Inuit settled.

    B. Kwakiutl settled.

    C. Seminoles lived.

    D. Pawnee lived.

SS4H1

Read the passage below and answer the following question.

> We the People of the United States, in Order to form a more erfect Union, estblish Justice, insure domestic Tranquility, provide for the common defense, promote the general Welfare, and secure the Blessings of Liberty to ourselves and our Posterity, do ordain and establish this Constitution for the United States of America.

59. The passage above is found in the   SS4CG

    A. Bill of Rights.

    B. Articles of Confederation.

    C. Declaration of Independence.

    D. Preamble to the Constitution.

60. John McCain and Barack Obama are running for president. The winner may serve no more than two terms. This is an example of   SS4CG3

    A. term limits.

    B. common good.

    C. popular sovereignty.

    D. overriding the president.

61. How did Lewis and Clark contribute **most** to western expansion?   SS4H6

    A. Their fearless stand at the Alamo eventually opened the southwest to expansion.

    B. Their journey led to other US citizens wanting to move west.

    C. Thanks to their discovery of gold, California became a recognized state.

    D. Their defeat of Native Americans opened territory for white settlers.

62. For centuries, the South focused on raising crops like tobacco and cotton. What is this called?   SS4E1

    A. specialization

    B. opportunity cost

    C. embargos

    D. free trade

63. North America's many forests and wildlife allowed France to make a lot of money from its   SS4H2

    A. lumber sales.

    B. fur trade.

    C. cotton industry.

    D. fishing markets.

Use the map below to answer question number 64.

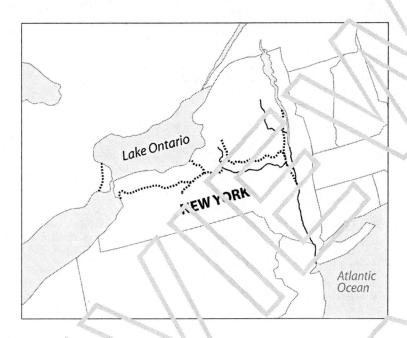

64. What does the map above **most likely** whow?   SS4G1

   A. Ohio River

   B. the Great Basin

   C. The Continental Divide

   D. Erie Canal

65. What was the **main**   SS4H5
    reason the Articles of
    Confederation failed?

   A. It gave too much power to the
      national government.

   B. It did not give enough power
      to the national government

   C. It did not give enough power
      to the local state governments.

   D. It gave too much power to the
      judicial branch of
      government.

66. Under the First   SS4CG2
    Amendment,

   A. citizens are free to express
      themselves in different ways.

   B. citizens have the right to carry
      a gun with them at all times.

   C. the government may establish
      a religion.

   D. the government can take
      property without paying for it.

67. The Sons of Liberty   SS4H4

    A. protested laws like the Stamp Act.

    B. supported British loyalists.

    C. fought in the French and Indian War.

    D. wrote the Declaration of Independence.

68. If Congress passes a law   SS4H5
and the president signs it,
the judicial branch can still
declare the law unconstitutional.
What is this an example of?

    A. separation of powers

    B. an amendment

    C. checks and balances.

    D. due process

69. Both the state of Georgia   SS4CG1
and the United States government have the right to impose
taxes. This is an example of

    A. reserved powers.

    B. delegated powers.

    C. limited government.

    D. concurrent powers.

70. Eli Whitney's cotton gin   SS4E1
made cotton processing
much faster and cheaper. What is
Eli's invention an example of?

    A. a technological advancement

    B. voluntary exchange

    C. an opportunity cost

    D. a price incentive.

Georgia 4 Social Studies Practice Test 2

The purpose of this practice test is to measure your progress in Social Studies. This test is based on the GPS-based Georgia CRCT in Social Studies and adheres to the sample question format provided by the Georgia Department of Education.

General Directions:

1. Read all directions carefully.

2. Read each question or sample. Then choose the best answer.

3. Choose only one answer for each question. If you change an answer, be sure to erase your original answer completely

Use the map below to answer questions 1 through 3.

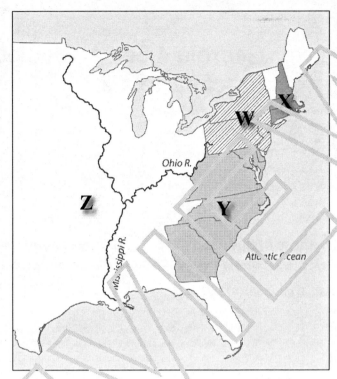

1. In which region on the map did shipbuilding and fishing become important industries? SS4H3

   A. W　　　　　B. X　　　　　C. Y　　　　　D. Z

2. The New England colonies are represented on the map by the letter SS4H3

   A. W.　　　　　B. X.　　　　　C. Y.　　　　　D. Z.

3. In which region on the map was tobacco an important crop? SS4H3

   A. W　　　　　B. X　　　　　C. Y　　　　　D. Z

4. Elizabeth Cady Stanton would have been **most** excited about   SS4H7

   A. the discovery of gold.

   B. women voting.

   C. the Great Compromise.

   D. the Underground Railroad.

5. What geographical feature did the British try to use in order to face the Americans in face-to-face battles?   SS4G2

   A. the Delaware River

   B. the Atlantic Ocean

   C. peninsulas

   D. open fields

6. Public education and the regulation of licenses are   SS4CG1

   A. reserved powers.

   B. delegated powers

   C. concurrent powers.

   D. rights in the Preamble.

7. When England traded with the American colonies, it was an example of   SS4E1

   A. voluntary exchange.

   B. a budget.

   C. the impact of technology.

   D. democracy

8. Which of the following is **not accurate** about the Alamo?   SS4H6

   A. Every Texan who fought at the Alamo died or was executed.

   B. The Mexican leader of the battle was General Santa Anna

   C. The Texans successfully defeated the Mexican troops.

   D. The battle happened because Texas wanted to be independent.

9. Who does the following list describe?   SS4H4

   - American soldier and commander
   - led the American victory at Saratoga
   - betrayed America and tried to give the British secret information

   A. Lord Cornwallis

   B. Benedict Arnold

   C. Patrick Henry

   D. George Washington

10. Which of the following is guaranteed under the First Amendment? SS4CG2

    A. Brian's right to vote.

    B. Christopher's right to drive a car.

    C. Martha's right to criticize Congress

    D. Eric's right to own a gun.

11. The Midwest Plains became home to the SS4H1

    A. Inuit.

    B. Seminole.

    C. Pawnee.

    D. Hopi.

12. If Mark wants to make sure that he spends less money than he makes, he should SS4E2

    A. apply for a loan.

    B. forget about saving

    C. work two jobs.

    D. make a budget.

13. Which natural feature links the Atlantic Ocean to the Great Lakes? SS4G1

    A. Erie Canal

    B. Atlantic Coastal Plain

    C. St. Lawrence River

    D. Continental Divide

14. Brian lives in Atlanta, GA. He stands on a corner and preaches against the war in Iraq. He wears a shirt that says "Peace not War". Brian is practicing his SS4H5

    A. First Amendment rights.

    B. Second Amendment rights.

    C. Nineteenth Amendment rights.

    D. Twelfth Amendment rights.

Read the list below and answer the following question.

- separation of powers
- checks and balances
- term limits

15. What is the best heading for the list above? SS4CG3

    A. Responsibilities of the President.

    B. Why Fiscal Policy is Important

    C. Ways to Limit the Power of Leaders

    D. Reasons for Having a National Defense.

16. Juan Ponce de Leon is **most** remembered for   SS4H2

 A. being friends with Native Americans.

 B. discovering Florida.

 C. exploring the St. Lawrence River.

 D. Establishing Hispaniola.

17. What was **most** important about the battle of Saratoga?   SS4H4

 A. General Washington defeated Cornwallis.

 B. It was the first time that American troops defeated the British.

 C. It gave Britain hope that it could win the war.

 D. America's victory convinced the French to help the revolution.

18. Which branch of government is responsible for making sure laws do not violate the rights of citizens?   SS4CG3

 A. legislative

 B. executive

 C. judicial

 D. the Senate

Read the list below and answer the following question.

- respect the rights of others
- obey laws
- community activism

19. What is the best heading for the list above?   SS4CG4

 A. Presidential Elections

 B. Natural Rights

 C. Reasons People Become Political Leaders

 D. Ways that People Practice Positive Citizenship

20. What contributed **most** to the development of mining towns in the west?   SS4H5

 A. the discovery of gold

 B. the relocating of Native Americans

 C. the discovery of oil

 D. the invention of the steamboat

21. In the US, most leaders are chosen by   SS4CG1

 A. natural rights.

 B. popular sovereignty.

 C. federalism.

 D. concurrent powers.

22. Who established Spain's first permanent colony in the Americas? SS4H2

    A. Juan Ponce de Leon

    B. Hernando de Soto

    C. Christopher Columbus

    D. Samuel de Champlain

23. The Lewis and Clark Expedition depended **most** on the SS4G2

    A. Rocky Mountains.

    B. St. Lawrence River

    C. Missouri River

    D. Mississippi River

24. Mary wants a job so she can buy a car. She finds a job, but she has to quit softball practice to be able to work. What is Mary's opportunity cost? SS4E1

    A. the cost of the car

    B. fun of playing softball

    C. getting a job

    D. There is no opportunity cost

Read the list below and answer the following question.

- Learned to grow crops
- Built houses using available resources
- learned to live in unfamiliar climates

25. What is the **best** heading for the list above? SS4G2

    A. Basic Habits of Nomadic Peoples

    B. Reasons for territorial expansion in North America

    C. Lifestyle of the Native American Plains Indians

    D. Ways European Settlers Adapted to Survive

26. Early Native Americans depended on the natural environment because it SS4H1

    A. protected them from droughts.

    B. allowed them to raise cash crops.

    C. provided food and shelter.

    D. taught them farming from Europeans.

27. The Three-Fifths compromise SS4H7

    A. established the legislative branch of government.

    B. allowed slaves to be partially counted as part of the US population.

    C. made George Washington president.

    D. allowed Southerners to count slaves in the population in exchange for ending the slave trade.

Read the list below and answer the following question.

- New England's biggest city and commercial center during the colonial period

- resisted British policies in the 1760s and 70s

- home to a lot of trade and commerce

28. Which city is the list describing? SS4G1

    A. Philadelphia

    B. Boston

    C. New York

    D. Chicago

29. A colonist living in South Carolina **most likely** relied on SS4H3

    A. fish markets.

    B. cash crops.

    C. fur trade.

    D. gold mining.

30. A positive character trait of good leaders is SS4CG5

    A. honesty.

    B. fear.

    C. selfishness.

    D. none of the above.

31. If the majority of the Senate and the House of Representatives passes a bill, it SS4CG3

    A. instantly becomes a law.

    B. must be signed by the president before becoming a law.

    C. is vetoed by Congress.

    D. is approved by the judicial branch

Use the image below to answer question number 32.

32. What event is **most likely** portrayed in the image above? SS4H4

A. the French and Indian War

C. the Battle of Yorktown

B. the Boston Tea Party

D. the Alamo

33. David wants to buy a new SS4E2
car. Since the car costs
more money than he has, David
pays for half the car out of his
savings account and borrows the
rest. David now has

A. debt.

B. a budget.

C. income.

D. savings.

34 Which of the following SS4H1
groups of people lived in
the northwest United States?

A. Seminoles

B. Pawnee

C. Hopi

D. Nez Perez

35. US citizens can not be forced to house soldiers during times of peace. Which amendment guarantees this protection? **SS4H5**

   A. Second Amendment

   B. Third Amendment

   C. Seventh Amendment

   D. Eighth Amendment

36. Natural rights are **SS4CG1**

   A. rights that promise happiness and good fortune.

   B. rights that people are born with.

   C. rights that the government can violate.

   D. rights that people are given when they turn eighteen.

37. Which of the following is an example of a price incentive? **SS4E1**

   A. a customer purchasing items with a credit card

   B. a hardware store increasing the cost of lumber

   C. an increase in supply and demand

   D. a department store putting clothes on sale

38. Why was slavery less important in the Middle and New England Colonies? **SS4G2**

   A. They relied heavily on cash crops.

   B. They were far behind the South in business and industries.

   C. They did not rely as heavily on cash crops

   D. Slavery was just as important in all colonial regions.

39. Descendants of the first people to live in the Americas are known as **SS4H1**

   A. African Americans.

   B. Native Americans.

   C. white colonists.

   D. Spanish explorers.

40. Native Americans who lived in forest regions, close to rivers, or along coasts, often **SS4G1**

   A. established permanent settlements.

   B. lived nomadic lifestyles.

   C. relied on the buffalo for food.

   D. relied on deserts to survive.

41. In the United States, The national and state governments both have power to govern. This is called   SS4H7
    A. federalism.
    B. the Preamble.
    C. reserved powers.
    D. delegated powers.

42. The Puritan church was a central part of life in   SS4H3
    A. Pennsylvania,
    B. New England.
    C. New York.
    D. the South.

43. The Oregon trail was   SS4H6
    A. the secret route that led slaves to freedom.
    B. the route that many settlers followed west.
    C. used to move Native Americans to reservations.
    D. a famous route used for cattle drives.

44. What is best for society is often called   SS4CG4
    A. common good.
    B. a petition.
    C. federalism.
    D. democracy.

45. Which region did Hernando de Soto explore?   SS4H2
    A. California
    B. New York
    C. Georgia
    D. Canada

46. In which order did the following events happen?   SS4H4
    1. Saratoga
    2. Yorktown
    3. French and Indian War
    4. Lexington
    A. 3,4,2,1
    B. 4,3,1,2
    C. 1,3,2,4
    D. 3,4,1,2

47. Which branch of the US government is responsible for enforcing laws?   SS4H5
    A. legislative
    B. executive
    C. judicial
    D. the president's cabinet

Use the map below to answer question number 48.

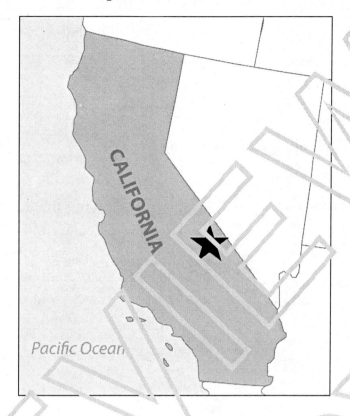

48. What does the star represent on the map?   SS4G1

    A. Lake Superior

    B. Erie Canal

    C. Death Valley

    D. Atlantic Coastal Plain

49. The system that allows power to be divided between two levels of government is called   SS4CG1

    A. federalism.

    B. popular sovereignty.

    C. fiscal policy.

    D. democracy.

50. The rules of society that citizens are expected to obey are called   SS4CG3

    A. rights.

    B. demands.

    C. laws.

    D. bills.

51. The search for gold and
the desire for land were
reasons that

SS4H6

  A. settlers moved west.

  B. Native Americans moved to
     Oregon.

  C. France bought Louisiana from
     the United States.

  D. Texans surrendered at the
     Alamo.

**Read the passage below and answer the
following question.**

In New England, fishing and
shipping were important. Rather
than try to produce everything, they
focused on these industries. This led
to more production and also
improved the standard of living in
the colonies.

52. The passage above is
describing colonial

SS4E1

  A. voluntary exchange.

  B. free trade.

  C. specialization

  D. supply and demand.

53. The money that workers
receive for their labor is
called

SS4E2

  A. taxes.

  B. income.

  C. price.

  D. monetary policy

54. After the colonies
declared independence,
they passed their first set of
national laws. What was this
document called?

SS4H5

  A. Articles of Confederation.

  B. Bill of Rights.

  C. Constitution.

  D. Electoral College.

55. Which of the following is
guaranteed under the First
Amendment?

SS4CG2

  A. Tracy's right to work from
     home.

  B. Jack's right to disagree with
     his state's Senator.

  C. Michael's right to own a gun.

  D. Mary's right to participate in
     elections.

56. The first European expedition to reach the Pacific Ocean was led by [SS4H2]

A. Samuel de Champlain.

B. Vasco Nunez Balboa.

C. Henry Hudson.

D. John Cabot.

57. Congress passes a law on immigration. However, the president does not approve the law and the bill dies. This is an example of [SS4H5]

A. separation of powers.

B. checks and balances.

C. legislative authority.

D. civil power.

58. What is **most** important about the St. Lawrence River? [SS4G1]

A. It allows boats to travel from New York to Chicago.

B. It is the longest river in California.

C. It connects the Great Lakes to the Atlantic Ocean.

D. It provides much of the Midwest with water.

Use this information to answer the question below.

Federalism

A. Delegated Powers

  1. raise an army

  2. sign treaties

B. Concurrent Powers

  1. _____

  2. build roads

59. Jenny is making an outline for her school report. Which of the following best completes her outline above? [SS4CG1]

A. carry on foreign trade

B. public education

C. regulate licenses

D. impose taxes

60. The steamboats' ability to make transportation easier and faster is one example of [SS4E1]

A. technology's economic impact.

B. specialization.

C. voluntary exchange.

D. the decline of business in the 1800s.

61. The first ten amendments to the Constitution are known as   SS4H5

A. checks and balances.

B. the Bill of Rights.

C. the Articles of Confederation.

D. compromises.

Read the list below and answer the following question.

- staying informed
- voting
- volunteering
- communication

62. What is the best heading for the list above?   SS4H5

A. Fiscal Responsibilities

B. How Citizens Take Part in Democracy

C. Duties of Government

D. Examples of Federalism

63. Who is most famous for exploring what is today New York?   SS4H2

A. Henry Hudson

B. Jacques Cartier

C. Hernando de Soto

D. Juan Ponce de Leon

64. "No taxation without representation!" was a protest against   SS4H3

A. colonial boycotts.

B. laws like the Stamp Act.

C. the Second Continental Congress.

D. the signing of the Declaration of Independence.

Read the list below and answer the following question.

- Make and enforce laws.
- Provide a national defense
- Manage money responsibly

65. What is the best heading for the list above?   SS4CG3

A. Responsibilities of the US Supreme Court

B. Power Given to the House of Representatives

C. Responsibilities of the National Government

D. Duties of US Citizens

66. How did the invention of the telegraph impact the United States?   SS4E1

    A. It did not impact the US at all.

    B. It allowed people to communicate with each other all over the country.

    C. It made long-distance trans portation easier and faster.

    D. It made many US citizens wealthy landowners.

67. The first military conflict of the American Revolution occurred at   SS4H4

    A. Lexington and Concord, Massachusetts.

    B. Trenton, New Jersey.

    C. Yorktown, Virginia.

    D. Saratoga, New York.

68. Which of the following did **not** happen at the Constitutional Convention?   SS4H5

    A. The Great Compromise established the House of Representatives and the Senate.

    B. The Three-fifths compromise stated that slaves would count as three-fifths of a person.

    C. The Articles of Confedera tion was added to the Constitution.

    D. Power was divided among three branches of government.

69. How did the French and Indian war help lead to the American Revolution?   SS4H

    A. It gave the French control over all colonists in North America

    B. It allowed the colonists to govern themselves.

    C. It led Great Britain to pass laws requiring colonists to help pay for the war debt.

    D. It angered Native Americans and caused them to leave the Union.

Read the list below and answer the following question.

- Freedom of the press
- Freedom of religion
- Freedom of speech

70. What is the best heading SS4CG2
    for the list above?

    A. Rights Guaranteed by
       the First Amendment

    B. Rights Guaranteed by the
       Third Amendment

    C. Examples of Checks and
       Balances

    D. Rights Guaranteed in the
       Articles of Confederation

CRCT

Please fill out the form completely, and return by mail or fax to American Book Company.

Purchase Order #: _____   Date: _____

Contact Person: _____

School Name (and District, if any): _____
_____

Billing Address: _____   Street Address: ☐ same as billing

_____   _____

Attn: _____   Attn: _____

_____   _____

_____   _____

Phone: _____   E-Mail: _____

Credit Card #: _____   Exp Date: _____

Authorized Signature: _____

Order Number	Product Title	Pricing* (10 books)	Qty	Pricing (30+ books)	Qty	Total Cost
GA3-M0607	Mastering the Georgia 3rd Grade CRCT in Math	$169.90 (1 set of 10 books)		$329.70 (1 set of 30 books)		
GA3-R0607	Mastering the Georgia 3rd Grade CRCT in Reading	$169.90 (1 set of 10 books)		$329.70 (1 set of 30 books)		
GA3-S0508	Mastering the Georgia 3rd Grade CRCT in Science	$169.90 (1 set of 10 books)		$329.70 (1 set of 30 books)		
GA3-H1008	Mastering the Georgia 3rd Grade CRCT in Social Studies	$169.90 (1 set of 10 books)		$329.70 (1 set of 30 books)		
GA4-M0808	Mastering the Georgia 4th Grade CRCT in Math	$169.90 (1 set of 10 books)		$329.70 (1 set of 30 books)		
GA4-R0808	Mastering the Georgia 4th Grade CRCT in Reading	$169.90 (1 set of 10 books)		$329.70 (1 set of 30 books)		
GA4-S0708	Mastering the Georgia 4th Grade CRCT in Science	$169.90 (1 set of 10 books)		$329.70 (1 set of 30 books)		
GA4-H1008	Mastering the Georgia 4th Grade CRCT in Social Studies	$169.90 (1 set of 10 books)		$329.70 (1 set of 30 books)		
GA5-M0806	Mastering the Georgia 5th Grade CRCT in Math	$169.90 (1 set of 10 books)		$329.70 (1 set of 30 books)		
GA5-R1206	Mastering the Georgia 5th Grade CRCT in Reading	$169.90 (1 set of 10 books)		$329.70 (1 set of 30 books)		
GA5-S1107	Mastering the Georgia 5th Grade CRCT in Science	$169.90 (1 set of 10 books)		$329.70 (1 set of 30 books)		
GA5-H0808	Mastering the Georgia 5th Grade CRCT in Social Studies	$169.90 (1 set of 10 books)		$329.70 (1 set of 30 books)		
GA5-W1008	Mastering the Georgia Grade 5 Writing Assessment	$169.90 (1 set of 10 books)		$329.70 (1 set of 30 books)		
GA6-L0508	Mastering the Georgia 6th Grade CRCT in ELA	$169.90 (1 set of 10 books)		$329.70 (1 set of 30 books)		
GA6-M0305	Mastering the Georgia 6th Grade CRCT in Math	$169.90 (1 set of 10 books)		$329.70 (1 set of 30 books)		
GA6-R0108	Mastering the Georgia 6th Grade CRCT in Reading	$169.90 (1 set of 10 books)		$329.70 (1 set of 30 books)		
GA6-S1206	Mastering the Georgia 6th Grade CRCT in Science	$169.90 (1 set of 10 books)		$329.70 (1 set of 30 books)		
GA6-H0208	Mastering the Georgia 6th Grade CRCT in Social Studies	$169.90 (1 set of 10 books)		$329.70 (1 set of 30 books)		
GA7-L0508	Mastering the Georgia 7th Grade CRCT in ELA	$169.90 (1 set of 10 books)		$329.70 (1 set of 30 books)		
GA7-M0305	Mastering the Georgia 7th Grade CRCT in Math	$169.90 (1 set of 10 books)		$329.70 (1 set of 30 books)		
GA7-R0707	Mastering the Georgia 7th Grade CRCT in Reading	$169.90 (1 set of 10 books)		$329.70 (1 set of 30 books)		
GA7-S1206	Mastering the Georgia 7th Grade CRCT in Science	$169.90 (1 set of 10 books)		$329.70 (1 set of 30 books)		
GA7-H0208	Mastering the Georgia 7th Grade CRCT in Social Studies	$169.90 (1 set of 10 books)		$329.70 (1 set of 30 books)		
GA8-L0505	Passing the Georgia 8th Grade CRCT in ELA	$169.90 (1 set of 10 books)		$329.70 (1 set of 30 books)		
GA8-MATH08	Passing the Georgia 8th Grade CRCT in Math	$169.90 (1 set of 10 books)		$329.70 (1 set of 30 books)		
GA8-R0505	Passing the Georgia 8th Grade CRCT in Reading	$169.90 (1 set of 10 books)		$329.70 (1 set of 30 books)		
GA8-S0707	Passing the Georgia 8th Grade CRCT in Science	$169.90 (1 set of 10 books)		$329.70 (1 set of 30 books)		
GA8-H0607	Passing the Georgia 8th Grade CRCT in Georgia Studies	$169.90 (1 set of 10 books)		$329.70 (1 set of 30 books)		
GA8-W0907	Passing the Georgia Grade 8 Writing Assessment	$169.90 (1 set of 10 books)		$329.70 (1 set of 30 books)		

1-5-09   *Minimum order is 1 set of 10 books of the same subject.

Subtotal

American Book Company • PO Box 2638 • Woodstock, GA 30188-1383
Toll Free Phone: 1-888-264-5877 • Toll-Free Fax: 1-866-827-3240
Web Site: www.americanbookcompany.com

Shipping & Handling 12%

Total

Call Toll-Free 1-888-264-5877 to ORDER and for FREE PREVIEW COPIES!
Visit americanbookcompany.com to download FREE SAMPLES of all of our products!